Be More Human

'This book is brilliant. Tony is a hero with such an important message to help us connect with a more natural way of living, so we feel happier and healthier'
David Flynn and Stephen Flynn, the Happy Pear

'That Tony so wholly and passionately walks his talk is the real key here – you're not witnessing marketing spiel, you're witnessing a living, breathing, thriving example of unsullied human nature. It should be the norm, but given how far removed we are from our nature – it's become extraordinary'
Eminé Rushton, author and journalist

'Tony exposes you to the areas that have been compromised by modern living and aren't serving you; suggests small changes that can be implemented for big impact, even in the busiest of lifestyles. Keep spreading the word'
David Haye, former unified Cruiserweight World Champion and World Heavyweight Champion boxer

'The irony of our hyperconnected world is disconnection from that which is most important. In *Be More Human*, Riddle challenges us to mend this wound by enriching our natural and ancient relationship with that which is fundamental: our relationship with others, the natural environments we share and, of course, ourselves. Extending from there, this inspiring read will teach you the importance of movement, sleep, community, conscious parenting, and even play – so we can together navigate the complexity of modern life with deeper meaning and greater purpose'
Rich Roll, author of *Finding Ultra*

An ultra-endurance athlete and Natural Lifestyle Coach, Tony Riddle garnered brilliant press coverage for his barefoot run from Land's End to John o'Groats, raising awareness and funds for sustainability and environmental NGOs. In September 2021, he broke the men's running record by completing the 400-plus miles of the Three Peaks challenge barefoot in 9 days, 7 hours and 44 minutes.

Be More Human

How to Transform Your Lifestyle
for Optimum Health, Happiness
and Vitality

TONY RIDDLE

PENGUIN LIFE

UK | USA | Canada | Ireland | Australia
India | New Zealand | South Africa

Penguin Life is part of the Penguin Random House group of companies
whose addresses can be found at global.penguinrandomhouse.com.

First published 2022
001

**The information in this book is not a substitute for and is not to
be relied on for medical or healthcare professional advice. Please consult your
GP before changing, stopping or starting any medical treatment. So far as the author
is aware, the information given is correct and up to date as at the time of writing.
The author and publishers disclaim, as far as the law allows, any liability
arising directly or indirectly from the use or misuse of the
information contained in this book.**

Text design by Alice Woodward
Typeset by Jouve (UK), Milton Keynes
Printed and bound in Great Britain by Clays Ltd, Elcograf S.p.A.

The authorized representative in the EEA is Penguin Random House Ireland,
Morrison Chambers, 32 Nassau Street, Dublin D02 YH68

A CIP catalogue record for this book is available from the British Library

ISBN: 978–0–241–50959–3

www.greenpenguin.co.uk

Penguin Random House is committed to a
sustainable future for our business, our readers
and our planet. This book is made from Forest
Stewardship Council® certified paper.

Contents

Preface

It's 2014 and I'm standing in the disused London to Scotland railway ticket hall that I have spent the last few years converting into my gym. Around me are my trainers, coaches and movement specialists. Around me I can see the product of my life's work and the realization of my dreams. I'm teaching a class about being more human and how to move the body as nature intended. It's a philosophy I've been developing and living for decades. I should feel complete . . . but I don't.

Suddenly, a train thunders overhead. As the gym is attached to a railway platform, this isn't unusual. All day, every day, trains hurtle past, rattling the equipment and vibrating the floor. It's an event so commonplace that no one really pays attention to it. Yet something about this train, at this time, hits me – hard. A feeling of momentous awakening cuts me off mid-sentence and almost knocks me over. It's as though my entire life has been building to this very second. As the noise and vibration grow more intense, shaking the walls, the strip lighting flickers and the bars on the window tremble. Somewhere deep inside, I'm hit with a sudden bolt of clarity. Standing silently in front of my gym class, I feel like the train is thundering into the depths of my unconscious and I begin to see my life, and the memories and stories I've told myself, flash before me. I see the lack, the untruths, the struggles and frustrations. And finally, I arrive at the impossible truth: I was a fraud. I had been conning everyone, and worst of all, I had been conning myself. It was time to wake up.

For all my trying, I was not healthy or content. How had this happened? I had been striving for conventional success my whole life. I believed that owning a business, a house, a car and having a family would bring me happiness. I'd followed the socially accepted steps towards success, embodied the conventions: gone to school, a stint in the army, become a personal trainer, a Pilates teacher, a movement coach, set up my own gym. I'd 'made it', lived and breathed the Human Laboratory – and yet it wasn't working. I'd watched my friends, family and community comply and suffer the same challenges, yet I still believed in the promised satisfaction that complying should bring. So, why did I feel so unsuccessful when, really, I'd 100% achieved what from the outside looked like the definition of 'success'? Yes, I'd built a business, bought a house, had a family. But I felt like a failure. I couldn't help asking myself, *was it just me who felt such disconnection?*

I had set up my gym to help people strip back their lives and live more simply, as nature intended. But, as the train rattled overhead, I had to accept that I was failing. And I had to question why. I had to strip back my pride and ego to reveal my true, vulnerable self. The train forced me to ask myself: what is it that makes a successful human in the modern world? I had to face up to the fact that it sure as hell wasn't what I'd been doing up until that point. I had been chasing the wrong sort of success – the money-driven, modern-world view, which takes no account of true wellness, emotions or spirituality, yet each of these is needed to be a healthy, happy and truly successful human being.

At my moment of realization, I was 38 years old and feeling the consequences of my own unnatural lifestyle. I owned a gym, yet my finances were in a mess. In recklessly striving to stay afloat and maintain the illusion of success, I barely saw my wife and two small daughters. Any remaining energy outside of that was being driven into pacifying drugs and drink to numb the guilt, shame and pain. I was living the antithesis of everything I believed in, and worse still, I was misguidedly teaching others to do the same. I had let all of my needs slip aside in the pursuit of what I believed to be 'success'.

There I was, in an artificially lit, underground room with poor air quality and filled with electromagnetic waves, espousing the pseudo virtues of rewilding in a completely unnatural environment that was in no way conducive to how human health works in nature. That day marked the beginning of my awakening. That train smashed through my fragile facade of success, exposing my hidden child self and his every unmet need. It knocked my ego into humility. Things had to fundamentally change.

Tony 2.0 in training

Today, I can see clearly that all this happened not *to* me, but *for* me. The old me was quite happy not voicing the full truth of my experiences. I was fine with carefully crafting my tale, filtering the less impressive parts of my story. I would skip over my long-suppressed guilt, shame, embarrassment. I was sparing with the truth: my childhood deformity, my suffering, the pain, aggression, self-harm, drugs, drink, prison, self-hatred, suicidal thoughts, divorce, losing my business and property, the bankruptcy and the breakdown. Before the health, wealth and happiness came a lot of stuff that I was never proud of.

It has been one hell of a process deconstructing my old self. Fortunately, I came to realize that I had to go through all of it to figure out who the universe had uniquely assigned me to be and how to be of service to others, as Tony 2.0.

Within a month of the train-induced epiphany, I had closed the gym and launched my broken and bankrupt self into what would become a year of immersive, soul-searching workshops, retreats, potent spiritual practices, truth-seeking and prolific reading. My breakdown-breakthrough provided the spark of recognition that I needed to make serious changes in my belief systems and my approach to life. I had to put in a lot of graft, internal deep diving, research, unlearning, relearning and experimentation to work out exactly what those changes had to be and to make them happen.

Even with all this knowledge, I was not walking my talk. Then I imagined how others were feeling. Those who didn't have the information or means of implementing it, those born into the compromised environment of the modern world with no way of knowing that natural health and happiness existed right there within their own being. Right there and then, those people – along with my two small daughters – became my 'why', the reason beyond myself to be the change.

So, that was the start of the breaking down of my belief systems. It also awakened an overwhelmingly empowering sense of my own ability to change. There was no place to hide. I could no longer justify following the expected, ego-driven route through life; I just wanted to be happy. It was time to get authentic. Be more human. Be the change. And so I did.

Rebooting, reconnecting, rewilding

The breakthrough was excruciating, terrifying. We were bankrupt. My body looked like I'd stepped off the cover of *Men's Health*, yet under my skin and muscles it cried for nourishment. My mind was running on overdrive, I had few supportive friends and barely saw my family. I was at rock bottom – not a comfortable place for a previously ego-driven man to find himself in. But I was going to relearn how to run barefoot along that rock bottom.

The breakthrough gave me an opportunity to reboot, reconnect and rewild; to put all the knowledge that I'd accumulated until that point – everything I knew but just wasn't living – into practice. I had been a data-gatherer. Now it was time to be hunter-gatherer, in search of a different kind of life template, to seek out the truth. What a blessing a blank canvas is! In my search for the solution, I was going to have to break away from convention and think differently, *inside the box* of the Human Laboratory. How could I upgrade my existing environment to make it work *for* my health and happiness, instead of *against* it? How could I be the change within my own communities? I was going to have to go far away. Possibly to the most remote corners of the earth and the deepest memories stored away in my childhood, to places where normality didn't involve a constructed acceptance of physical, emotional and spiritual maladies.

I would need to dig out the deeply buried seeds of wisdom that I had planted all those years before, as a barefooted boy, when I actively sought out freedom and risk in nature – times I felt most alive, most myself. Those seeds sent out shoots, developed a trunk, grew branches I could use to swing from my current existence into one of learning how to grow into a mature, living oak tree of fulfilment and wellness. I would have to establish my true needs and find a new tribe of influence that would help me grow through living, rather than misguidedly protecting me from it.

I began to take care of my physical body from a place of love and respect rather than from my ego. I began allowing it to function and move optimally, exactly how it was designed to. I also got curi-ous about my spiritual self, my social environment, the world around me – and how they all link together. I came to understand my strengths and blockages and shone a light on those areas that needed care and attention. Asking questions, allowing myself to experience the world and gathering my tribe all confirmed my innate knowledge that happiness has very little to do with the fleet-ing experience of pleasure, or the accumulation of stuff. Through these activities, I realized that success and happiness were only pos-sible when I was innately fulfilled.

I began to fill myself up from the inside. I found the places where inauthentic life had cracked me and I had filled the cracks with junk. I cleaned them out and refilled them with nature's nourishment. I stopped pursuing the illusion of happiness, desperately consuming instant, hollow pleasure. With big bright eyes, I began to seek inner fulfilment instead. Being authentically human isn't to be found in a pay cheque, a flash car, the external trappings of wealth and fame. If nourished correctly, it exists whether we wear designer labels, have a spouse and 2.4 children, or not. We have to shed the layers of artifice we have built up under the illusion they are protecting us. We have to *be more human.*

The reason I believe it is so important to share my story is because I wasn't always where I am now. It has taken me years of discovery, experimenting, reworking, changing paths, failing and recreating to get to this point. I am now delivering the answers and the impetus to you, so that you can experience for yourself the exultant joy and health that come from truly connecting to nature – and your human nature.

This new sense of empowerment is far beyond anything I ever felt in my life before discovering how to reconnect to the wild side of myself – the side that needs to eat, sleep, move, play and breathe the way my ancestors once did. It's like having access to the world through a fresh yet ancient sensory system. It's a process of rewilding and you are capable of it, too. When I say that you are one powerful human being, who has everything you need within you to be the change and alter your current state of mind, I mean it from a deep place of experience and authenticity. You are awe-inspiring. You are loved.

Introduction: How to be More Human

If you spend a lot of time in front of blue screen light, consumed and stressed by the 24/7 connectivity of modern technology, I see you. Tired but wired, relying on coffee, often ill, feeling disconnected from your body. You may be feeling lonely, lacking in direction and purpose. Maybe you have depression or an ever-present anxiety? It could be you're habitually overspending, or are necking a bottle of wine each night. Maybe you have a chronic condition, are overweight, have niggling injuries or an unhappy gut. Maybe your posture is making you look ten years older than you are? I know you.

These are just a few of the lifestyle-led conditions of our supposedly advanced society. Our dysfunctional behaviour is so ubiquitous that it's seen as normal, even glamorized. 'Meh, I'll sleep when I'm dead!' I've heard many a suited City worker utter as he sucks on the plastic lid of his third coffee of the morning. Why is it we've accepted this state of barely surviving, when we were built to thrive?

You may have picked up this book because you want to feel fitter and better in yourself but don't know where to start, or maybe you think you have no time in your busy life to prioritize wellness. This book will help you begin to make changes. No matter what our gender, age or background, we all have the same fundamental human needs. Only if these natural needs are met can we move from a protection state of survival to a growth state of thriving. *You don't need to exist in a perpetual state of 'making do'.*

I have followed many paths, often extreme ones, to refine my natural lifestyle philosophy, going where many would choose not to in order to uncover information and make it more available to others. I want to be the embodiment of holistic, natural living. As a father of four children, I feel the urgency for a change in our current disconnected behaviours. We need to do more to communicate the problems that arise from our disconnection from the natural world. So, I want to be an example to others of a truly healthy and happy human, and to make this way of life accessible to as many people as possible.

We are born knowing how to keep ourselves well and be happy. It is our consumerist, tech-driven, frantic societies that have swayed us from this innate wisdom and left us preoccupied with *wants* in place of true *needs* and fulfilment. This book is your route to 'rewilding' yourself back to your natural, healthy state.

When I first began my transformation from what I call a 'zoo' human to a 'rewilded' human, I noticed that the term 'rewilding' caused resistance in some of my clients who had no interest in being 'wild'. The indigenous people of our planet don't want to be referred to as wild, either.

Taken to its extreme, rewilding can be about living in a cave, foraging, tracking down prey, making tools and fire, building shelters, sleeping out under the stars and turning your back on modern society. There are a few within the rewilding community taking it to this level. This does appeal to the hunter-gatherer in me, but this book is not about demonizing city life to find wild wellness. I currently make good use of technology for all the wonderful ways it positively benefits my modern life. I enjoy living in a house with electricity and plumbing, and I spread my message by taking clients and working with companies in the City. But – and here's the distinction – I always ensure my wild human needs are met. I know that not everybody can connect with the term 'rewilding'. Just don't be afraid of it: this book is here to show you how to find your version of wild.

Rewilding – according to the *Cambridge Dictionary*
The process of protecting an environment and returning it to its natural state, for example by bringing back wild animals that used to live there.

Rewilding runs directly counter to human attempts to control and cultivate nature.

Rewilding – according to me
Finding ways of living that are more in sync with our human biology, with the goal of living more healthily and happily in the modern world and being more human.

Rewilding returns us to a more self-willed state and reverses the process of domestication.

From the ego-system to the eco-system

Rewilding is about taking an honest look at your life and asking the question, 'How could I upgrade my existing environment to make it work for my health and happiness instead of against it?'

Rewilding is about designing simple ways of living that create greater health and wellbeing for future generations and for our planet.

In essence, it's disconnecting from our 'ego-system' and reconnecting to our 'eco-system'. It's about reducing the focus on our superficial wants and desires and instead turning to the natural world for inspiration, sustenance and nourishment. To make positive changes towards your wellbeing, you can rewild your gut, diet, posture, exercise, sleep, community, home and even commute, and this book will show you how. None of this means having to go and live in a cave and hunt down your own food – unless, of course, you want to. Instead of telling you to change every aspect of your lifestyle, I'll show you how to connect with your innate, wild nature, which holds the key to finding true health and happiness. This book is a comprehensive guide to everything I've learned and all that I've seen working with my rewilding clients throughout the last decade.

Rewild your own way

I made a commitment to myself and my family to be the change I want to see; to lead the way in rewilding my life and helping others in turn, so we can all know how it feels to live as nature intended. I want to make sure that future generations never need to rewild again. I'm here to show you how you can really, truly thrive to your fullest potential! In sharing my belief with you in ancestral wisdom and what works in nature, I'll help you relearn to reconnect with consciousness, with yourself, with your tribe, with the earth. You'll be taking on the powerful responsibility to start thriving, not just surviving.

This book presents to you my tried-and-tested methods for implementing doable, small steps while enjoying big shifts in your mindset, motivation and perceptions. Over the following chapters we will navigate the biology of your body and mind as they are now, in your compromised modern state, and find out how you naturally want to be and how we can get you there in the most efficient way possible.

In creating a happy body and an environment more conducive to your wellbeing, your mind will find clarity, calm and happiness, and your body will follow its lead. I've packed in my experiences on my own journey as well as the most incredible transformations of my clients, plus everything I learned from diving head first into my childhood conditioning to release hidden traumas, patterns and beliefs.

How to use this book

Part One introduces you to the concepts of reconnecting, rewiring and rewilding with nature. It asks you to do the mindset work necessary for behaviour change and will give you all the understanding and inspiration you need to make your own natural lifestyle upgrade.

Part Two shows you how to become more human in practice. We'll focus on five key areas of everyday living:

- **Breathing and Being**
- **Moving and Playing**
- **Eating and Drinking**
- **Sleeping and Resting**
- **Outdoors and Indoors**

Each of the key areas introduces easily accessible exercises, activities and techniques. At the end of each of the five practical chapters, you'll find my simple foundational steps for rewilding and tips for how to introduce nature into your existing lifestyle for ultimate, incremental gains.

The conclusion of *Be More Human* is anything but an ending. Here, you'll find a whole range of useful takeaways, referencing other sources and places to go as you attempt to become and stay more human.

When you have a really busy schedule, the information and tips provided for you within this guide, although simple, may seem overwhelming; the last thing you need is to introduce *more* to an already oversubscribed day. I get it: I'm a husband, a father, I have two businesses to steer and have lived between two countries. This book shows you how to change incrementally, changing your beliefs and habits in small ways bit by bit, to completely overhaul your health and happiness.

20/80 wisdom

A great piece of coaching wisdom I learned from one of my own mentors, barefoot running coach Lee Saxby, is the ability to focus on the 20% input needed to create an 80% improved output. Honing in only on what is absolutely necessary for healing a particular problem results in maximum efficiency. This golden nugget of 20/80 wisdom can be applied to any transformational process – so you can rewild your behaviours and see improvements to your wellness with minimum effort.

I encourage you to adopt the 20/80 approach as the most productive way to make nature gains in your fast-paced urbanite world. Rather than attempting to squeeze out time you don't have and uploading information into your overstimulated brain that won't make any tangible difference, the 20/80 approach means you take on only what you need; this influences the bigger picture without wasting energy.

What I mean by 'the bigger picture' is that you start to view your world differently. As you're only uploading 20% into your system, that 20% must allow you to gain the skills to establish your own filter to determine what is useless 'stuff' and what is nourishing. You'll learn to regularly ask yourself: 'Is this going to project me into the amazing, crystal-clear state of conscious growth that Tony keeps going on about?'

Do your daily uploads

Take the six to eight hours of usable time you have during your day (yes, you really do – how often do you pick up your phone without thinking?). Instead of attempting to add 'rewilding' to your already packed to-do list, we find ways to attach rewilding tools to the things you're *already doing* during those hours: breathing and moving. You start to see time differently and take opportunities as they appear: maybe practise your ankle mobility during a conference call, incorporate some wild play into your walk home with the kids, or even whip your shoes off and ground barefoot in your garden each morning. These are simple uploads that are easily tagged on to your day.

I don't need you to read this book in order from cover to cover (unless you want to!). You might decide to dive straight into working on rewilding your movement, because that's where your immediate interest lies – great! Spend a week, a month, however long you need, focusing on how to incorporate better movement into your day. Then pick your next area and do the same there.

These daily uploads then become habits – your new norms – almost seamlessly. And because such rewilding gains have a telescopic effect on your days and sensibilities, their benefits are multiplied the more of them you implement.

It becomes a positive cycle: the more incredible you feel from these small uploads, the more excited you'll be to add more into your day. Before you know it, you will be living your days in a state of thriving as your new norm and excitedly seeking more opportunity for growth – increasingly energized, more empowered, inspired and radiating good vibes more vivaciously than you ever expected. Don't be afraid to start small, begin with what you can and only do what you can turn into a habit.

Be more human

I'm not promising you an easy ride. It will be confronting at times, frustrating and emotional, too. There may be emotional and physical discomfort, but that just means you're getting deep into the good stuff! If you commit to the basics, you will emerge from your experience like a butterfly from a cocoon as an authentic version of yourself, astounded at the capability of your body and mind. You'll discover a way of life that, once experienced, you'll never want to lose.

As you work your way through the book, you'll become familiar with the comprehensive range of rewilding tools and techniques at your disposal. You'll see that you can implement them within your current environment, allowing your urban mind to settle and the warrior within to emerge.

Now, with a thundering high five and a big bear hug, let's do this!

PART ONE
Reconnecting with Nature

Humans are the most advanced species on the planet. Yet we are so far from functioning at our best. Stressed. Overworked. Tired. Anxious. Injured. Addicted. Ill. The pressures and constant hustle of our modern world have detached us from the way we are supposed to live, connect and thrive. While we've come to accept these afflictions as part of the way we live our lives, they are far from natural. We don't need to put up with them.

Our collective illness is a result of us losing something that is critically important for our wellbeing and that of our future generations: **a connection with nature and our natural habitat**. Over time, we have become domesticated and disconnected. Although we're no longer living in caves, our wild human is still within us and it has fundamental needs.

Nature has planted these precious seeds of opportunity within us, starting with our basic physiological, social and spiritual needs. In order to survive as a human animal, we need air, shelter, sleep, food, water, sunlight, movement and human contact. To *thrive* as a human animal, we require nourishing environments, the opportunity to breathe clean air, sleep deeply, eat nourishing food, drink fresh water and soak up the optimum direct sunlight. We need to reconnect to natural movement and experiential play.

In Part One we're going to focus on our **Physical**, **Social** and **Spiritual** needs. Although examining these separately, there will be lots of crossover, as they all work together for our wellbeing.

In Chapter 1 we'll look at how our physical needs are not being met by our current lifestyles. I'll show how modern wellness is failing us and focus on how to live more naturally, by drawing out the ancient wisdom of our bodies.

In Chapter 2 we will examine how our mindset is shaped by the people around us – our tribes of influence. Our environment – and who we share it with – is crucial to our understanding of the world and how to navigate it. We may need to unlearn some inherited behaviours to progress to new, improved ones that better serve us. This chapter will show you how.

In Chapter 3 we'll try to better understand our human spiritual needs. My philosophy teaches one-consciousness and how to find connection to the earth, the plants and animals. This chapter will focus on helping you find inner peace and focus through ancient and wild techniques.

Let's go!

CHAPTER 1

Living in Nature – How We Move Determines How We Feel

Well, well, unwell?

At this stage of our evolution, we human beings are striving for ultimate wellness to the point of desperation. We're looking in all the wrong places to fill voids; seeking support in gurus, television shows, TikTok. Meanwhile, we get sicker, bigger, more tired, frustrated and anxious. The global wellness industry is booming. Yet:

- Worldwide obesity has nearly tripled since 1975 and now kills more people than hunger.
- Suicide remains the most common cause of death among men under 50 in the UK.
- Globally, around 280 million people of all ages suffer from depression.
- 40% of disability worldwide is now attributed to depression and anxiety.

All the official governing bodies in charge of these statistics maintain that these conditions are preventable. There's a gaping chasm between our understanding of and desire for wellness and our ability to actually achieve total, maintainable health of our bodies, minds and spirits.

We are innately wild, connected and empowered beings. If we could just wake up, break out and relearn how to live in nature.

We go against nature, we go against ourselves

Somehow, humans never manage to satisfy our insatiable materialistic wants. We continue to fell forests and pollute the air, soil and water, lurching from climate crisis towards species extinction. All we have to show for our endeavour are piles of inorganic rubbish. Day after day, more of our precious natural world is being consumed and destroyed by our disconnected, disrespectful, disconcerting ways. Habitats and those that inhabit them are being abused by our relentless appetites. Addicted to plastic products, we are biting off the hand that feeds us: *'It's okay, we can grow an artificial one.'* All the evidence suggests we're prepared to sacrifice it all for a moment's pleasure. We feel we control, rather than are part of, the ecosystem. It's time that we understand how wrong this assumption is – how connected we are supposed to be.

Only 4–5% of mammals on this planet are wild, with the rest zoo-caged or farmed. This is the same percentage as the number of indigenous peoples vs the rest of the world's human population. Through habitat loss and shocking abuse, the indigenous defenders of our natural world are fighting for their rights to survive. Indigenous people protect 80% of our world's biodiversity. If this 5% are protecting 80% of global biodiversity, what is it that the rest of us are doing? The more we connect and appreciate nature, the more we might want to protect what we have, before it's too late.

We are physically *part of* nature, so why do we go *against* nature? How do we reconnect? How do we rediscover how to live like human beings were meant to live?

We go towards nature, we become more human

The most obvious and effective way is to get out there! Nature immersion studies report how we can use the restorative powers of nature to heal the stresses and strains of our modern-day, urbanite malaise and improve physical and cognitive health. Numerous studies highlight the benefits of natural healing sunlight on our skin and our eyes, explaining how sunlight supports our circadian rhythms, synthesizes vitamin D3, lowers cholesterol and produces that all-important happy hormone, serotonin. Others link nature walks with better mental health. Reconnecting with nature for just 20 minutes a day enhances our human experience, lowers heart rate, blood pressure and stress hormones, boosts immunity and enables us to thrive. Moving through nature – with an upright posture and, ideally, connection to the ground through bare feet – literally nourishes our mind and body. *Being* nature as opposed to *being in* nature is our ultimate human state.

WALKING NATURALLY

Natural walking emphasizes nasal breathing (see page 51), posture and being hyper-aware of our natural surroundings. Lift your chin and chest as if you're looking at the horizon, open up your field of vision and get your bare feet on the forest floor (or any natural surface will do if you're not near the woods!). The more wild, sensory skin you have in the game, the better your experience.

Scientists are now discovering that the trees in forests are communicating all the time, with each other and with the soil, in an interconnected invisible conversation. When we walk naturally through those forests, we are part of that communication, inhaling and absorbing the experience through our senses. We are as close as it's physically possible to be in this microbiome of organisms. We are breathing in the terpenes: the aromatic compounds of the forest.

When we inhale forest air, we breathe in phytoncides, plant-emitted airborne chemicals. Phytoncides possess antibacterial and antifungal properties that help plants fight disease. When we inhale them, our brains and bodies respond by increasing the number of a type of white blood cells called natural killer cells. These cells can kill tumour and virus-infected cells in our bodies. *Shinrin-yoku*, meaning 'forest bathing', is a practice that came out of Japan in the 1980s. It encourages people to get outside in the forest to unravel the stresses and strains of their urban experience and improve health. In one study of forest bathing, increased natural killer-cell activity from just a three-day experience lasted for more than 30 days afterwards. Researchers are currently exploring whether exposure to the forest and nature's potent healing powers can help prevent certain cancers.

Healing the mind through the senses

When we move through a forest, we are being hit with nature's nurturing aromatherapy cabinet, stimulating our senses and triggering a response. We absorb the experience of nature immersion through touch, sight, smell and taste – a full sensory experience, feeding our neural pathways, rewiring and rewilding.

Within the modern convenient urban environment, we live and work in linear rooms, with thick manmade materials insulating our feet from feeling the ground beneath us; we are experiencing, inhaling and absorbing, but with as little natural expression as possible and barely any sensory stimulation: headphones plugged in, blasted by artificial lights and air-conditioned air. We are depriving ourselves of the sensory experiences that trigger the phenomena of neuroplasticity and neuromuscular activity.

Neuroplasticity is your brain's ability to rewire itself when it recognizes the need for adaption. Through certain stimuli we can continue to rewire and develop throughout life. Without sensory uploads our rewiring and development are stunted and stagnant and our brain is unable to develop through adulthood.

To find physical balance and stability, and perform the most basic of human movements, our brains and bodies need proprioceptive ability – the awareness of where we are in space. Our modern life, our clothing and gadgets and the ease of convenience they present can block this opportunity for growth; we become divorced from stimuli – from feeling and sensory perception – and our human being is stunted as a result.

We can bring that natural connection back. Here are a few examples of how:

- Remove your feet from your proprioception-blinding shoes and make tactile reconnection to the natural world through your bare skin.
- Rewild your hyper-visual screen-time eyes by reconnecting with your panoramic visual field to fully scope your environment.
- Disconnect from the hustle to reconnect to the sounds of nature. Immerse your ancestral ears in nature's sounds; you may be surprised by just how much you can hear in your surrounding area, once you tune in.

How about adopting nature's norms?

People who consciously align with the natural order of all things will be most 'successful' at being human. If our needs aren't being met, we are suffering. The more we suffer, the more pacifying wants we reach out for, to fill the void of our natural needs. Electronic calming natural scenes and waterfall screensavers may induce a synthetic rest-and-digest state, the soothing parasympathetic nervous system. But it doesn't actually *physically connect us to nature* or make us aware of our role within nature, by which I mean to always be conscious, kind and live alongside our environment, without harming it.

Making natural lifestyle changes has a much bigger-picture impact on your daily life than you might think. When we do so we nourish our whole frequency, which has a ripple effect on all our interactions. This can only lead to a better connection with ourselves, other living beings and our planet.

After going through my own environmental and socially induced sickness and coming out the other side as a conscious man, I knew I needed to address the cataclysmic problem of modern-day ill health, disaffection, suffering, addiction and depression. Challenging societal constructions can not only save us money and energy, it's also incredibly liberating – mentally, physically and emotionally – and heals us of anxiety and malaise.

My natural lifestyle philosophy is a way to recharge, reboot and reconnect the modern human, to re-align ourselves with nature and the fact that *we are nature*, for improved emotional, spiritual, physical and social health. This is about deconstructing the ways of living within our everyday habitats that simply aren't serving us, or allowing us to reach our human potential and thrive as conscious, connected beings. You'll find plenty of ways you can make small changes to your life in Part Two of this book. Rather than seeking to remove us from our modern, urban habitats, my approach is to shine a light on how to form functional and healthy ancestral habits, whatever environment you're in.

A PRINCIPLE FOR LIVING

We can't all live in nature, but we can learn to live more naturally
We don't need to go live in a cave or up a mountain; anyone can start living more naturally within the context of their own life, whatever and wherever that is . . .

CHAPTER 2

Living in Tribes – Our Community is Our World

Let me begin by asking you:

- Are your lifestyle choices serving you?
- Are you being your best representation of yourself?
- Are your lifestyle choices setting a good example for future generations?

What comes to mind when you think about tribes? Perhaps simplistic, culturally reductive images like the ones I used to hold: feathered headdresses, jungle huts, hunting barefoot, bows and arrows, wild dancing, drumming, chanting and casual nudity. 'Tribe' was a word that suggested 'uncivilized' people inhabiting the most remote corners of the earth. My white, colonial-influenced lens ensured I looked at tribes with curiosity, fascination, suspicion and probably fear. I scorned the magic of tribal people, from my lofty privileged position. I dismissed their shamanism with cynicism and their intellect as primitive. The indigenous existence seemed to 'lack' the comforts, education and opportunity that I, living in the Western world, experienced. It was a misguided and ignorant opinion to harbour, tucked away in the depths of my consciousness, especially for someone who had never even visited a tribal community or sat down with a tribesperson.

I was simply showing my conditioning, which extended to everything I assumed in my entire life, my compartmentalized views of the world. This conditioning gave me structure: I knew what my life was supposed to look like, how I was supposed to feel, what I was supposed to achieve and, most importantly, what I needed to do to fit in and be 'normal'. How do we wind up indoctrinated with so many unquestioned beliefs?

Your perception of normal, like mine, has been shaped by the templates of your own tribe's perception of what normal is. When I use the term 'tribe', I am referring to your social network: your family, friends, teachers and community. I use the term consciously, with intention not cultural appropriation, to look to the deepest essence of what it is to be human.

We become a direct reflection of our tribe's social behaviours through a process I call 'normalizing', or 'tribal thinking'. Deciphering the intricacies of our own individual templates – the beliefs, behaviours and traumas bestowed upon us by our tribe – is perhaps the most important initial step to successful rewilding. These templates inform how we see, interpret and respond to the world. Without understanding the roots of our limiting beliefs, how can we expect to heal them and rebuild ourselves – and our children – on stable foundations?

How did we get here, to our current state? Instead of a race of thriving beings at one with ourselves, each other and with nature, we've normalized surviving in a cage of anxiety, depression, disease, stagnation and general malaise, using drugs, alcohol, junk food, shopping, TV, smartphones and other forms of constant disengagement and distraction.

> We were once the connected, but now find ourselves needing to reconnect.
>
> We were once the wild, but now find ourselves having to rewild.
>
> We were once born with the most immense power, but now find ourselves having to become empowered.
>
> We were once born free, but now find ourselves having to fight for our freedom.
>
> We were born equal, but now we are having to fight for equality.

Let me introduce Bruce Parry. When I met him, we discussed his recent stay with the Penan tribe, a nomadic people indigenous to Sarawak and Brunei in south-west Asia, one of the last remaining tribes of hunters and gatherers. Bruce is a documentarian, author, explorer, trek leader and indigenous rights advocate. He applies an ethnographic filter through which to observe the tribes he studies and spends time with. As you can imagine, he has explored many an extreme environment, lived with previously untouched, remote indigenous tribes and exposed many of the planet's most important environmental issues.

Bruce told me that the Penan are an egalitarian tribe with no leaders: all equal, equal as one, equal with nature. They don't have to deal with the strains of inequality. They don't have to worry about the problems of hierarchy and the injustice that comes with value judgement, as everyone is treated the same.

But it isn't just the Penan tribe. The Mbendjele in the Congo is another egalitarian tribe, living and thriving without leaders. While in the developed world we have been led to fear 'anarchy' without leadership and hierarchy, tribes like the Mbendjele and Penan thrive on it.

CEREMONIES FOR EQUALITY

The Mbendjele tribe in the Congo perform a playful dance and song called Massana. All the women, young and old, make fun of the men. The playful act is a form of teasing out antisocial behaviour within the group. Men who have been aggressive, disrespectful or even lazy lovers are humorously, but assertively, held to account by the women in the communal space. In a non-hierarchical matriarchy, the women embody their own quality of collective power to keep balance.

The men have their own playful ceremony called Ejengi. A huge straw figure – Ejengi – is created to symbolize the alpha male, who is rejected and pushed out of the tribe to bring back the female and male harmony. In addition, any of the tribe who show up with their ego, perhaps postulating that they are the best hunter, will have their tools/weapons taken away and are ignored until they are prepared to drop the competitive ego mindset and return to the oneness of the tribe.

Who is your tribe of influence?

If we want to understand social behaviours around us, it's crucial to recognize our own belief systems and patterns of thought and behaviour. If they're holding us back, we need to challenge them.

It is our responsibility to do the inner work to dismantle old compromising ways so that we can preserve our connected, wild, innate abilities and grow into empowered beings. We need to demonstrate appropriate behaviours and create appropriate environments, so that upcoming generations can establish their human needs to thrive. Let's protect our endangered natural state of being from becoming more 'zoo'. I am talking about all us adults here, not just the parents among us. These are all our children. As the old Nigerian proverb states, 'It takes a village to raise a child.'

We're often blindly guided by 'social norms', but at what cost? We have to take more responsibility for what 'normal' means. We have to look at what it is to be a human animal, to understand that living a fulfilled life on this wondrous planet means normalizing natural movement and being for growing children.

Our childhood experiences – how safe we feel, how connected we are to our caregivers – shape our adulthood. We become aware of the scars from our disconnected past and childhood trauma unavoidably plays out in our adult years: if our fundamental needs aren't met, we inevitably suffer and this suffering emerges in later years – as emotional or physiological distress. If, as an able-bodied child, your movement spectrum is deprived as you grow up and you aren't naturally encouraged to move enough, your physiological framework may be impacted, and so too could your neurology. If your digestive system isn't nurtured, then your ability to absorb nutrients may be compromised, which affects your mind, body and biome. If your sleep habits and habitat aren't nourishing your growth, then this will influence your mind–body relationship.

'What we call civilization demands the denial of human needs.'

Gabor Maté

We learn our lifestyle habits through observation, seeing what is modelled by our caregivers. Let's turn to the work of child development expert and physician Gabor Maté. Maté is renowned for his studies which prove that it is only within a state of suffering that humans develop addictions. His work shows that differing modern habitats and social differences instigate the childhood traumas that exist at the root of human suffering, and are responsible for creating a need for distraction from this suffering through the development of addictions. Maté has placed particular responsibility for the plague of suffering and addiction in modern society on the dysfunction of the modern human community, what I call our 'tribe of influence'.

The contemporary version of our tribe of influence is not supporting our growth, as is so evident in my own story. We may live in the Human Zoo, but we *can* unlock the internal cage and create space that encourages the ability to thrive – even in our urban settings – while still ensuring that our biologically normal, physical, social and spiritual needs are met.

We are the only species that chooses to lock ourselves away from nature. But we can tap into ancient wisdom, transform our norm, realize our potential and relearn how to thrive. The ultimate gift for the next generations is to dismantle and deconstruct our inherited templates that aren't serving us, so that the next generations aren't inheriting what won't serve them.

This does not mean demonizing our own tribes of influence; they were and are doing the best they can with what they inherited. This is about honouring the past with compassion, while walking the honest path of growth, so that future generations can inherit templates that are better for humans and better for the planet.

You can't go back in time to change what you were or weren't exposed to as a child, but you absolutely can do the inner work to make peace with your early traumas, dismantling inherited behavioural templates that no longer serve you. You can 'choose' to live authentically.

> 'Be more concerned with your character than your reputation, because your character is what you really are, while your reputation is merely what others think you are . . . the true test of a man's character is what he does when no one is watching.'
>
> *John Wooden*

Our actions really do count. The next generations are observing us, emulating us. So, let's show them how to be more human. Let's all take on the responsibility of shaping a better future.

Childhood trauma and how it shows up

From the last trimester in the womb to seven years of age, our emotional brain and imagination brain are being formed. These developing young beings are absorbing our pasts and recording their futures. In these earliest years, they are walking around in a permanent state of meditation, where their experiences will ultimately shape the lens through which they see their world, their future. The tribe of influence that surrounds us shapes our physical, social, spiritual and emotional development.

Up until seven years of age, children's brains are said to operate at the same frequency that we as adults can only reach in meditation or in deep sleep. From the ages of two to seven, children are primarily in Theta brainwave cycles of around four to eight cycles per second. This is a super-imaginative, absorbent state, which allows the child to programme their mind, form their templates and learn everything they can about the world around them. People under hypnosis and animals share this Theta frequency.

From the ages of five to eight, brainwaves transition to Alpha frequency. Children operating at this frequency are moving seamlessly between their imagination and their external reality and haven't yet developed much capacity for critical thinking, allowing for powerful creativity to function without interruption. They are operating from their subconscious minds. The same brainwave state adults enter into in meditation is the permanent state for children at this age. They don't need to take themselves off to a meditation cushion and set aside formal time to enter it. The first six years of life are quite literally spent in hypnosis. This lack of ability for critical thinking means that, as children, we are programmed passively as we don't have the ability to consciously choose or reject behaviours and beliefs imparted to us by our tribe.

Once we hit the age of seven and upwards, we enter into Beta state of around 13 cycles per second. With this comes the maturation of our conscious and analytical minds – we can understand and employ logic, focus deliberately and root deeply in the belief systems we inherited during our first six years, be those positive, inclusive and creative beliefs, or limited beliefs about ourselves and others. This is where we are to spend most of the rest of our lives.

Free to learn

As children, we enter the education for our long, adult lives. Formal education, that is. Sitting in classrooms for anything between 10 and 15 years of our development. But what if this formal education actually goes against our natural human needs? What do we learn? That being chained to a desk or a workbench is our lot in life? What if we were free to learn our own way?

LEARNING MINDSET

As you move through this book, re-child your absorbent mind and return to that playful state of mind where you have a heightened desire to learn. Take a moment to breathe, to pause and to rediscover those pangs of excitement of what it was like to come across something that you were really passionate about. Think about a book that changed your life when you were little; you were absorbent then, now channel that feeling.

Psychologist Peter Gray's book, *Free to Learn*, examines how important it is to align our movement, play and sleep with our natural needs. Nothing of this is found in formal education. Gray interviewed ten leading anthropologists, each of whom had observed hunter-gatherer cultures in various isolated parts of the world across three continents. Every single anthropologist said that the children, including young teenagers, were free to play and explore on their own all day long, without any adult guidance. Tribal adults let the children play freely because they know it is how they learn the valuable skills they need to develop in order to grow successfully into adulthood.

Without adult intervention, in three different geographical locations, they all had the same behaviours around play. Rather than sit through an education system, they are *acting out* what it is to be adults and learning what it is to be human. Compare the play habits of hunter-gatherer children with our own and there is a sharp awakening as to how far removed we are from how play works in nature. With his data, Peter Gray was able to show that the relationship between declining social skills and underdeveloped creativity in youngsters was down to the reduced amount of free play. Gray's data also demonstrates that, in line with declining child-led play since the 1950s, there have been notable plunges in empathy and creativity. Childhood mental health conditions including depression, anxiety and other stress-related issues have significantly risen.

Western children spend less than one waking day each week playing. Hunter-gatherer children of today are playing freely from the time they open their eyes in the morning until they close them at night. All day, every day, they are left to explore the far reaches of their imaginations and movement capacities without interruptive demands to sit still and be quiet, or to freeze their creativity and form an orderly line when a bell rings out across a playground. Their adult tribe members stand back and allow the natural phenomenon of play to unfold. Even into their teenage years, hunter-gatherers can be seen accessing their play state and building the foundation for their higher learning to acquire the physical, social and spiritual traits and values that characterize their culture.

Play *is* education: for socialization, for adult living, rather than as a means of programming workplace drones. A number of the anthropologists in Gray's study also noted that the children they observed in these cultures were among the brightest, happiest, most cooperative, most well-adjusted and resilient children that they had ever observed. From a biological, evolutionary perspective, play can be identified as nature's means of ensuring that young mammals (including young human beings) gain both the skills and the healthy character traits that they need to develop successfully and happily into adulthood.

A PRINCIPLE FOR LIVING

Reassess our habits: let's make our natural biological norms our social norms

Whatever has happened in the past, you have an opportunity to reset things and bring them back into alignment with your 'being' nature.

CHAPTER 3

Living for Meaning – Why Spiritual Connection Matters

Peace, oneness, connection – however you describe it, spirituality means different things to different people. One way we can connect spiritually is by establishing rituals, exploring ancient rites of passage. In Western culture, many of our rites of passage have long been removed, but this doesn't mean they aren't important. I've learned to reclaim many powerful practices as rites of passage, from reconnecting to myself through silent retreats or plant medicine ceremonies, to climbing mountains barefoot, immersing in ice baths, or simply relearning to build and make fire that needs to burn all night. This chapter delves into how we can tap into our spiritual core, and why this is so important for our wellbeing.

I go wild swimming in a cold lake every day: it enables me to find serenity. I see the cold water as a hit of adversity that helps me find the state of inner calm and become more resilient. The cold is a form of reboot, so I can find comfort even in uncomfortable situations. It helps me get clarity on the bigger picture, the modern malaise we all live with. This helps me see perhaps that that irritating email or phone call isn't really that stressful.

By practising how to remain calm in the ice-cold water, through accessing my down-regulated breathing practice (see below), I can tap into that same soothed state for the stressful call or email. I can simply 'be'. This complete sense of being aligns with being at one with nature. And who better to inform me of that than our ancestors, who traversed millions of years of intricate, phenomenal evolution to become strong, competent, courageous beings.

PREPARE TO STEP INTO COLD WATER

Cold-water immersion doesn't have to be in a lake or an ice tub, you can do it in a bath or shower. If you're feeling anxious about getting into the cold (or feeling anxious in any situation), use breathing to prepare you for the stress. This breathing practice is a way of **down-regulating your nervous system** (see page 47) to induce calmness and enter your rest-and-digest state, where you feel safe and protected:

- Take a deep inhale, then exhale fully before taking an inhale through the nose, and then as you enter the water fully exhale.
- Extend your exhale so that it's longer than your in-breath, repeating this breathwork practice as long as you remain in the cold water.
- Inhale, then lengthen the exhalation, as you down-regulate to move through the perceived threat of the cold.

Let's return to the Penan tribe. In Bruce Parry's descriptions of the tribe, he asserted that they operate as if in sustained meditation. From this, we can fairly assume that, to achieve their trance-like state of flow and oneness with their environment, they have naturally 'stretched' this childhood time spent in Theta frequency far into adulthood. This oneness comes from having played at being the animals they see every day, played at being the rocks, the plants, the sky, fire, water, even the weather. In this way, hunter-gatherers perpetuate one-consciousness through forging intrinsic connections with things outside of themselves. Modern urbanites are shortening this time in childhood and therefore augmenting their disconnection from oneness, making it harder to reintroduce it later in life.

When Bruce first met the people of the Penan tribe, he was instantly captivated by their ability to be 'at one' with the forest. They existed in and moved about in a profoundly crystal-clear state of being. Only when the tribe senses threat do they revert to protection mode, in total alignment with how it works in nature. So, what is so different for the Penan people that allows them to thrive effortlessly in a permanent space of growth, without the need for reciting mantras, keeping a gratitude journal or implementing a formal meditation practice?

The needs of the Penan tribe are met by the humble, symbiotic understanding and close relationship they have with their natural environment and one another – by being part of an interdependent, egalitarian tribe. This tribe IS nature. They are not separate from it, they are the ecosystem itself. It's a frequency so high that we urbanites can only reach it for fleeting moments, or through meditation. The Penan are in a permanent state of meditation, constantly wiring and rewiring both hemispheres of their brain through being at one with one and all. Bruce told me that although he classed himself as spiritual, he'd felt like an awkward Englishman among the tribe. He'd presented a mask for humour, banter and poking fun, and they were entirely without masks. Bruce told me that the tribe 'felt so themselves' because, compared to him, 'they were complete, in many ways that I wasn't complete, they had a deep sense of belonging.' More than that, 'they knew who they were in relation to place, in relation to their ancestors in that place, in relation to the other people alive today, in that place, and in relation to their children who will continue to live in that place.' Bruce went on to suggest that these tribes 'were free in a way that we aren't free, because they were known completely by everyone'. Bruce was implying that, despite their changing environment and threats to their survival, these contemporary hunter-gatherers didn't have to put on masks for the sort of anonymous urban life that we live, when we are always shifting between identities or pretending to be someone else. What's the point in pretending when you've been deeply known your whole life by everyone around you?

In many ways, this sense of deep belonging may always elude us in a fast-paced urban world. But we can choose to consciously seek that connection. Create space for more human chemistry, in real life, not on screen. Hug more. Listen without just waiting for your turn to speak. Breathe deeply. Break down grudges and barriers that may have been erected over years. It's not realistic to expect to live like the Penan, but we can learn from their system and apply it in micro form to our own existence.

Rites of passage

Let me tell you the story of Yehudi, an 80-year-old man I've been working with for many years. The day before Yehudi came on a workshop with me, which would involve him immersing in an ice bath, I had to spend an hour on the phone to persuade him to attend. You see, when Yehudi was born, he had stopped breathing, so they put him on a cold slab and blasted him with oxygen. His birth resulted in Post-Traumatic Stress Disorder that manifested in a terror of the cold. When he did finally turn up, he was among the first to get in the ice bath. And when he did, he let out a massive primal scream, a huge guttural roar resonating from deep within his body. Putting himself out there with all his vulnerability, he finally had an awakening years after his birth trauma, in this ice bath rite of passage.

Yehudi now does cold immersion as part of his morning routine, five times a week, in the early morning, all year round. He goes to the ponds in Hampstead or the River Lea in Hertfordshire. Western conventional wisdom tells us that we get more niggles, tension, pain and fatigue as we age, but this isn't the case for Yehudi. He is getting younger, more energized and is now in his best self through reconnecting to ways of living that are more in sync with our human nature. Yehudi is not only providing his children and grandchildren with a better template for how an 80-year-old can move, he is demonstrating how it is never too late to make the change. Yehudi messaged me to say thank you for his initiation. One icy morning, immersing in the River Lea, he had finally found peace. (We'll get back to Yehudi in Part Two. He can tell us something about the power of movement.)

Plunging into ice baths has become a modern-day rite of passage, an awakening. Awakenings help us see beyond our limitations, what has been normalized; if your individual consciousness changes then your reality changes too. Initiations and rites of passage reconnect us to the collective, the whole.

Yehudi waiting that long to exorcize his trauma and to finally find peace reminds us how important it is to take stock at various points along our journey to feel into how we're living: are we surviving or thriving?

Health and happiness and the ability to thrive are available to each and every one of us, but we are searching for them in the wrong places. To provide false contentment, we binge on alcohol, drugs, laboratory food, shopping, video games, nail bars and social media accounts depicting superficial covetable lives. These quick fixes are just further distractions from the truth. Not one of them is a growth-promoting, biologically normal call to be present.

A way into authentic being through Ayahuasca

Let me tell you about a potent ceremony I undertook with the plant Ayahuasca. During this experience, I reconnected with my masculine archetypes of the Magician and the Warrior, which would then later enable me to become a barefoot endurance athlete.

First, a bit about Ayahuasca. Put simply, it's a psychoactive brew originally used by indigenous tribes of the Amazon basin for spiritual and ceremonial purposes. Managed properly by trained shamans, imbibing the brew quickly affects the central nervous system, leading to an altered state of consciousness that can include hallucinations, out-of-body experiences and euphoria. Remember we have to be careful appropriating rituals which aren't from our own culture, always considering place, intention, due respect and reverence. I didn't do it lightly. I researched it and made sure I was with the right people, at the right time, in the right place.

Let me take you there . . .

I can feel the medicine way before the ceremony has even begun. The room is set and there is only one person between me and the shaman. There's one candle for us to see when we are each called to come up, to kneel and take a drink of this incredible teacher plant, Ayahuasca. Then the candle is blown out and we sit in the dark. To step aside, surrender and remain open to the process I introduce my 100 cycles of alternate nasal breathing, I wait for the force of the mother to enter. I don't have to wait too long. Before drinking the medicine, we are asked to set an intention. Mine is to discover freedom. The medicine comes in strong for me. I switch to deeper inhales and longer exhales. With every extended exhale my ego dissolves, my masks removed. I gain an ability to see consciousness as a tiered experience. It's as if I can see a grid of consciousness in the room. Somehow in the darkness, I can see each individual and where they are on their journey. Suddenly, this understanding of the pedestals and hierarchies around wealth and success dissolves for me. I get beyond a blockage I once had, where I would see people of certain success or wealth or fame as different to me. But here we are, millionaires, billionaires, celebs and Tony, all as one. It becomes evident that actually they aren't very successful at all at being human, because they aren't physically prepared. With this comes the message that, to be of service, you have to be the example. As if some magician energy is entering, I can now 'teleport', and find myself seeing the room through the eyes of the shaman, but from where he is sitting in the room. I suddenly have a huge tribal headdress made of feathers and it's as if I am holding the whole room. I am holding this space in my hands, my strength is holding the space in the room.

I am excited by this magic, to feel like a magician, to have these superpowers. But then the voice comes in. It's the ego and the immaturity of 'fuck, I didn't know we could do this!' Then, boom! my moment of self-congratulation has removed me from the divine momentary experience.

I find myself back in my position, where there is only one person between me and the shaman. I go back into my intention and slow and steady breathing, but now start to down-regulate my breath with long, slow and steady exhales – the breath I have discovered that enables me to access the medicine so cleanly. Now, I can feel as if I have a huge fur cape wrapped over my shoulders – I am a warrior and my warrior energy demands that I sit up strong and tall in the ceremony. It's in this moment that the boots I had to wear as a child come into my thoughts – the braced boots used to prise my congenital club feet to a position where it was perceived for feet to be normal. The message is clear and defined – to access the warrior, you have to lose the shoes. Up until this point, Tony the 43-year-old has parked his club foot somewhere way down in the vaults of traumatized inaccessibility. But, here in the medicine, the boots come in and so do the trauma and the emotion of it all. If I want freedom, I will have to let the trauma go. The trauma is my saboteur, inhibiting me from accessing my warrior superpowers. The finding of my breath helps me deconstruct the trauma within the ceremony.

As I bring my attention back to freedom, a very clear female voice enters with these words: 'We are born free, freedom is innate in all of us. But we are handed all this stuff, taught all these limiting and disempowering beliefs, all that keeps dragging us out of freedom, distracting us from being. We are born with all this amazing gear, yet we have no idea how to access it, because we have been given all this external distraction. It's okay to have material things and knowledge, but one should not be attached to these things, as the attachment is a further distraction from you – your being. But the thing about freedom, Tony, is that your freedom can be taken in a moment.' And then, suddenly with that last sentence, the medicine stops working.

Afterwards, I sat for hours in the dark while everyone else was still deep in their process. This was my last ceremony with Ayahuasca. I felt that the lesson had been about not becoming too attached to the medicine. I would now find this same depth of knowledge through my own superpowers, be it through refining the Magician or the Warrior energies I found in the ceremony, or through my breath. All to help me navigate my path and be of service to others.

Spiritual running

You may have picked up this book as you are a follower of my ultra-endurance events, which are the zenith of what can be achieved through following my natural lifestyle approach. My runs have become a spiritual, out-of-body experience, the Pilgrimage. As I neared the limits of my endurance during my 'One Man, Two Feet, Three Peaks' run, these words entered my thoughts: 'You are literally being reborn with every step.' With these words came the tears, but they were tears of joy. In breaking down the old, it was as if each and every step forward became the new. From this pilgrimage came the understanding that each step we make should be a step to finding our authentic self.

On another occasion, I could feel the trees moving with me as I was running. I was at a point of exhaustion, on the brink of being broken. The trees were still until I became level with them. Then I could feel my ancestors come to run with me. Strong, lean Celts, they were on each shoulder. They were also in the trees – they *were* the trees. The hairs on the back of my neck and the top of my head were fizzing as their words arrived: 'You are never alone, Tony.'

A PRINCIPLE FOR LIVING

Our spiritual journey is about thriving together, not surviving alone

We are not alone. Part of nature, we tread our path alongside other beings, animals, plants, trees and the earth itself, interdependent, all with our ancestors looking over us.

PART TWO

Being More Human in the Wild

The last three chapters have got you thinking about reconnecting, rewiring and rewilding. I hope it's given you the chance to reflect on the three key pillars of your life: your physical, social and spiritual wellbeing. Now you have that knowledge, it's time to put it into action. It's time to **be more human** in practice.

We will be focusing on five areas of your everyday living:

- Breathing and Being
- Moving and Playing
- Eating and Drinking
- Sleeping and Resting
- Outdoors and Indoors

This next part will have you rebooting your life for good. Each section will introduce easily accessible practices, activities and techniques. At the end of each of these practical chapters, you'll find my foundational steps for rewilding and tips on how to bring nature into your existing lifestyle. Let's go!

CHAPTER 4

Breathing and Being

'Noses are for breathing, mouths are for eating.'

Lola, my daughter

Lola's simple statement brings us right into the core of my beliefs about breathing. If you take this on board, you're on the way to greater wellbeing. But, before we get into the practicalities, and the various exercises that you'll learn throughout this chapter, let's look at why breathing is so vital to us and how a more natural approach to breathing can help us in so many wonderful ways.

There are many breathing techniques for a wide variety of needs and issues: from insomnia to waking in the morning; from boosting us in the afternoon slump to dropping us into rest in the evening; for mindful eating; to immerse in nature; for exercise; for alleviating asthma and a plethora of other ailments. Some powerful breathing practices even allow us to reach heightened psychedelic states and others help us to dismantle and deconstruct our trauma.

As you read this, how, exactly, are you breathing? In and out through your nose, with your lips closed? Or in and out through your mouth, not using your nose at all? But isn't breathing something our bodies do for us automatically? Yes, but by paying attention to it, we can intervene and consciously use breathing to benefit our health and wellbeing.

Your nervous system response

The incredible thing about breathing is that it's an immediate way we can actively influence our nervous system, without adding any extra things on your to-do list. You're breathing *anyway,* right? So if we can optimize our breathing habits, it brings us closer to the hunter-gatherer meditative state of being in our urban existence more often. How we do that? Our nervous system works in two parts: it goes up, and it goes down, according to what's happening around us. Throughout the book you'll hear me talking about **up-regulation** and **down-regulation**.

UP-regulation: sympathetic nervous system –
fight, flight or freeze

This is our body's stress response, of which we'll read much more throughout these pages. In fight, flight or freeze your body is primed for action, ready to run from a bear, anxious, stressed – but also excited. There are times where up-regulating can be a powerful tool, to prepare for an event, a talk, etc.

DOWN-regulation: parasympathetic nervous system – rest and digest

This is the ultimate skill to develop to influence everything else in this book and includes slowing your heart rate, lowering your blood pressure, calming your nerves. This is the zone we need to be in to be able to connect to nature and our innate human nature. Here's how:

BREATHE AND REBOOT ON THE HOUR

While nomadic tribes exist in their meditative states of being, this is the potential natural norm for us, too. We can remind ourselves to breathe and reboot our being. We can flip our mind from being full to being mindful. Through rebooting breath practices we can alter our perception of the environment we inhabit and find calm.

- Every hour, reboot the breath for 1 minute.
- Start by relaxing the space around your pelvic floor and lower abdomen (we're all so tense down there, learn to let it go). Then, inhale through your nose for 4 seconds and exhale out the nose for 6 seconds. Repeat this for 6 rounds, for every waking hour.

BREATHING TO CHANGE YOUR VIBES

One autumn evening, I spent hours on my own, in the woods, up in a tree, from sunset and into the depths of darkness. I relaxed, cleared my mind; the forest accepted me. I became transparent. Transparency is a skill that, once honed, is freedom in itself. Only then do you get to see nature in all her glory.

While tuning into the frequency of it all, pheasants came to roost all around me – on the forest floor and in the trees above me. What happened next was profound, demonstrating to me how independent of nature our thoughts can often be – the very saboteur of being.

Up in the tree, I congratulated myself. I hadn't moved a millimetre, not one noise had left my body, only the frequency of my thought, as in that moment of congratulation – 'Tony, aren't you wonderful for having all these pheasants around you' – I slipped out of divinity, out of my own interpretation of the Penan tribal frequency.

Then, with a sudden commotion in the trees, the pheasants were off. This was a powerful learning experience for me, one I will remember for ever. Ever since, I've introduced breathwork into my nature immersion practices for others to experience.

It is incredible how nature will expose herself from behind the veil. On another occasion, sitting at the lake at 42 Acres, a retreat in Somerset, breathing 100 cycles of alternate nostril breaths (see page 49), then pausing to sit, I could hear squeaking and scurrying at the edge of the lake. Something was heading towards me through the long grass. Suddenly, two young weasels popped out in front of me. I stayed humble with the breath. In return, I was able to witness them playing rough and tumble. It was as if they were oblivious to me; I was invisible. This experience highlighted what I had already suspected – that, once we drop into the being of nature, we will be gifted. With breathwork, we can disconnect from the ego system and reconnect with the ecosystem.

DROP INTO THE CONSCIOUSNESS
FREQUENCY OF ALL BEING

Here's some help to be grateful in nature. By combining nature immersion with breathwork, we can radically transform our stress-induced urbanite frequency in a much shorter time frame. I recommend alternate nostril breathing. This is a great practice to bring our attention to being in nature and disconnecting from the ego to reconnect to the eco. My advice with this practice is to think of inhaling nature as becoming the frequency of nature. Our left nostril stimulates the right (feminine) hemisphere of the brain and the right nostril stimulates the left (masculine) hemisphere.

- Allow your breath to settle by taking a long exhale, then place your thumb or forefinger on your right nostril and breathe into your left nostril. Pause, cover the left, and breathe out through the right. Then breathe in through the right, cover, breathe out through the left. You can change each round, or work in sets.

- Complete 10 cycles starting with the right nostril, 10 cycles with the left nostril and repeat until you hit up to 100 cycles of breath. Don't get wrapped up in how long you inhale or exhale for; it's far better to maintain a cycle that's comfortable, keeping relaxed in the pelvic basin, lower abdomen, shoulders and jaw. If you feel tension or your shoulders popping up at the end of the inhale, then lower the intensity.

Many ancient natural breathing techniques have been passed on to us and we're awakening to them and becoming aware of their ability to really empower us. Wim Hof, or 'The Iceman', has popularized breathing techniques and cold-water immersion, and other practices, which have the power to improve our immune systems and even cure serious illness. Just look at the world records he set for spending 1 hour, 53 minutes and 2 seconds immersed up to the base of his neck in an ice bath, or for running a marathon above the Arctic Circle in just a pair of shorts, or across the desert with no water. It's all incredible. So, that's what happens when we get it right. But what if we get it wrong?

When do we mouth breathe?

When we become stressed or anxious, we use quick, shallow breaths to get as much oxygen into the lungs as possible. Observe your own activity and you'll find yourself doing it. In his book *Breath*, James Nestor experiments with mouth breathing by taping his nose closed and recording the results. They showed a huge spike in his heart rate and blood pressure, signalling that the body had entered a state of stress. His body temperature dropped and his mental capacity was greatly reduced. When he went back to nasal breathing, his body returned to normal resting readings.

- Try covering your mouth and breathing through your nose for 1 minute. Notice any changes in your body?
- Set a timer to go off every hour and, when it does, record how you were breathing: nose breathing or mouth breathing?
- Remain conscious of your breath, being aware that constant mouth breathing can cause negative results for some people.

Mouth breathing is associated with obstruction of the nasal airway and is common among patients seeking orthodontic treatment. How did many of us become chronic mouth breathers? According to the great work of anthropologist and dentist Weston Price, it started going wrong when our diet went from natural to processed:

- Price served as head of research for the National Dental Association. He was interested in diet and its effects on growth and development.
- In the 1930s, Price studied cultures not yet exposed to a Western diet of processed foods: groups of Inuit, Pacific Islanders, Australian Aborigines, New Zealand Maori, Swiss Highlanders and South American Indians.
- Price observed that their children had broad faces, wide dental arches, aligned teeth and no tooth decay.
- Within one generation of consuming white flour, sugar and other nutrient-poor foods, faces became narrower, dental arches irregular and they began to develop crowded teeth and decay.
- Price put this down to poor nutrient absorption interfering with growth and tooth development.
- He also posited that this change in dietary habits encouraged the development of allergies and nasal-airway obstruction, causing mouth-breathing, a change in tongue posture and the associated development of a long and narrow face.

The power of nasal breathing

We can reboot our mind and physiology through nasal breathing. Choosing to use different modalities of breath can also help to dismantle and deconstruct the food groups you're addicted to, like sugar or fat. When we're up-regulated – in a stressed nervous system state – we often choose food to deal with the suffering. A pacifier for many, food has been used as a manipulative tool by parents, often as a distraction from pain. Unfortunately, this distraction means we then have to rewild our gut and our hearts, to relearn our true emotional needs. If we learn to recognize that we're up-regulated, we can down-regulate through breath, which in turn helps step outside the suffering, enabling us to alter our perception.

Something quite remarkable can happen

I'd read all the science I needed on nasal breathing – how the miracle molecule nitric oxide, produced through nasal breathing, acts as our body's first defence against airborne pathogens; as a vasodilator, dilating blood vessels throughout the body, reducing blood pressure and redistributing blood flow; and as a bronchial dilator, enabling my lungs to become more efficient at absorbing oxygen. All helping me to ultimately become a super-efficient, aerobic badass.

I started taping my mouth to rewild my breathing pattern back, but disappointingly my running pace dropped from an 8-minute-mile marathon to a 10-minute-mile marathon. Intuitively, I knew that if I respected and trusted the process, I would become the process and my being would be rewarded.

Once I surrendered to the process, I allowed my breath to determine my pace – no heart-rate monitor, no pacemaker, just trusting the breath. If I pushed too hard, I'd want to mouth breathe, so I'd slow up to get back to the nasal breath. Then, boom! I found myself reaching 8-minute miles while nasal breathing. I even found I could run marathons without water and food. (It turns out you lose 42% more water when you mouth breathe.)

I felt like I'd developed some superpowers, but not just from lowering my heart rate and blood pressure and my lungs becoming more efficient at absorbing oxygen. I had started to access some quite profound, heightened states of consciousness while running. Deep meditation. A 6-hour run became an opportunity to reach Nirvana. I had learned about the Tarahumara (Rarámuri) running people, a group of indigenous people from Chihuahua in Mexico, who see long-distance running as something transgressing a physical experience. I felt closer to their consciousness.

I started to see how being barefoot, my feet were a conduit, plugged in and grounded. By further rewiring my mind and body connection loop with the breath, I was entering a trance. One step. One breath. I could start channelling the most profound lessons, just as I had in the ceremonies of shamans.

Be your own breathwork guru

My own breathwork practice started seven years ago. Over time I have built up a collection of breathing exercises for different situations. These are laid out at the end of the chapter for you to practise whenever you need them. Previously, I'd used my breath as more of a controlling mechanism, a way of creating tension as my Pilates vocabulary told me. It certainly didn't have anything to do with letting go or empowering. This changed when two women walked into my coaching room and told me about a man called Alan Dolan, known as the breath guru, and how they'd had the most profound experience with him.

Katarina and I arrive early at the Idaba Yoga Centre in London to attend what is to be a transformational breath workshop with Alan Dolan. We are two of 50 people attending the workshop. Alan describes how he discovered transformational breath after trying many forms of meditation to reach the profound state of Nirvana. He'd be sitting for 30 minutes to access it and sometimes never get even a brief look behind the veil. Yet, with the breath, he would reach this profound state within a few minutes. This, of course, excites the room. After a quick demonstration of how to breathe and where to breathe into, Alan instructs us all to lie back. I listen to the cues of picking up the breath and dropping off the breath, picking up the breath and letting go. Some music starts and that is it for me. I go off into a deep meditation space. If a psychedelic experience and a profound meditation had a baby, this would be their love child. I suddenly start to feel movement in the room, a shift of energies around me. I can hear the music coming in again. Alan guides us to take our time to sit up. I am a little confused, assuming we're having a break. This surely can't be the end of a 3-hour workshop. But it is. Three hours have just disappeared in a breath. I look around the room and see disbelief, a vacant WTF look of astonishment on the faces of the 50 attendees. Alan asks if Katarina is okay. Oblivious to me, she has apparently had a really tough time. She isn't alone. As people start to share their experience, it becomes evident that this whole process has been quite extraordinary. It shows me that a simple practice of breath can enable us to get to the cause of our suffering, deconstruct and dismantle trauma or release emotional blockades. So exciting for the be-more-human movement, this is a way of accessing our true sense of being.

TRANSFORMATIONAL BREATH

First named by Dr Judith Kravitz in the mid-1970s, from her breathwork designed to release various traumas sustained by women during childbirth. Wanting to make it more effective and longer-lasting, she developed Transformational Breath as a technique to work on physical, emotional and spiritual levels. Based on an increased oxygen intake, this practice can help with feeling more in control and less susceptible to stress and anxiety.

Finding my voice

I used to have difficulty speaking publicly. To help me find my voice, a friend recommended that I see the crystal healer Abby Dixon, in Ibiza. In Abby, I found a kindred spirit. She had packed up a life in London, where she'd worked in human rights, and explored the world, before settling in Ibiza to teach yoga and perform poetry and sing. During her travels, Abby had learned a great deal about yogic practice, shamanism, crystal healing and sustainable living.

When I arrive at Abby's house, I find her sitting by the pool at a huge mandala and with her crystals set around her. As soon as I sit down, Abby says, 'Tell me about your voice. Close your eyes and tell me the first thing that comes to mind.' I close my eyes and visualize my parents taking me to the doctor when I was a small child. I was late to start talking and they wanted to know what was wrong. The doctor decided it was because my sister kept talking for me and I was just being really efficient. He concluded that I'd be ready to talk at some stage and left it at that.

Suddenly, I'm transported back to the hospital and having my support boots prised from my club feet to have my plaster casts removed and replaced, a process they repeated every week. I was screaming in pain but nobody was listening. Eventually, I gave up screaming, and talking. As I'm remembering all of this, Abby is placing crystals all over me and specifically on my throat. I relax completely and am drifting off when suddenly I hear the voices of all kinds of animals. Peacocks, dogs, a whole chorus of voices, 'We're just waiting to hear from you. It's your turn to start speaking.' My response: 'What the . . . ?!' I can feel a sensation building around my throat; Abby is removing the crystals from me. The crystal from my throat has become really hot. It is said that when the throat chakra is blocked, we struggle to communicate or can be fearful about speaking our truth. I felt I had experienced some profound reboot. We come into this world making lots of sound, and then our tribes of influence will often spend a lot of time telling us to sit still and be quiet. As I sit up, I'm blown away by how well I feel. I can't believe it. 'What is going on?' I ask.

That experience with Abby empowered me to find my voice. It wasn't only that I was speaking more, I was being invited to speak more too: talks, workshops, taking part in podcasts. Yet I had to go through such a huge dismantling process to get to my voice. It gifted me with this deep understanding of being down-regulated and really present.

My superpowers

By the time I returned home, I'd made the decision to run 879 miles from Land's End to John O'Groats, barefoot. I would lose my shoes and find my freedom. I soon came to understand that it is those early experiences that prevent and inhibit us from accessing what the universe has uniquely assigned for us. That these rites of passage provide the opportunity to have a rebirthing experience, one that serves to highlight or – better still – motivate us to let go of all that isn't serving us. Previously, I bought into the notion that I had to buy all the gear. Then, through these rites of passage, I woke up to discover that we *are* the incredible gear. Our bodies are all we need.

The run

A run, for me, is an opportunity to really be out on my own with no distraction other than just the breath. One step, one breath, one step, one breath, tuning in and being rewarded with some incredibly profound insights. It's not surprising, then, that a run, an event, becomes very much a 'pilgrimage'.

Like each one of these events, a run is a way of demonstrating the fullness of human potential. It also creates a huge platform for me to raise awareness of this potential, as well as the bigger picture around it. Each event is about sustainability in terms of the impact we're having on the environment, especially when it concerns raising awareness for indigenous people of the planet through Survival International, as the Three Bare Peaks Challenge did.

With each event I do that showcases human potential, I am effectively putting my whole practice under scrutiny. On the Land's End to John O'Groats run, Dr Rangan Chatterjee came out to interview me and said, 'Tony, you're really putting your lifestyle on the line, you know?' And that can be quite challenging. *What if you don't succeed? What if you break down?* At its core, success is about having unflinching confidence in these practices. One step, one breath. I park the ego. It's very much 'This is within me.'

Any run or event demonstrates different elements of my practice and the techniques I teach others – all of which you can find in Part Two from page 43, to see how you can incorporate them in your own way into your life. I can run that level of mileage, because of my movement practice, my play practice, my sleep, my rest. The way I eat and the way I hydrate all go into an event. In preparation I build up my training progressively, but then walk straight into the event like it's another day. The day before the Three Bare Peaks Challenge, I even did a summit of Snowdon. I ran barefoot up Snowdon and down again in 1 hour and 53 minutes. Starting the very next day, I ran it again as part of the challenge, then ran for 52 miles afterwards – all through building, building, building.

The specialist training builds on the basics that underpin my daily life: the ground living practice that helps nourish my running posture; the sleep, by creating an environment that enables me to sleep and be growth-promoting; the intuitive eating (see page 147). Due to the distances involved in the Three Peaks Challenge, I consumed more calories (two marathons a day add up to a lot of mileage). The physiology can handle it, the technique can handle it, but the body needs fuelling. In training, I was fasting, then going out and running. That's my rhythm – like hunting: move first, hunt, eat. However, there is always the danger of a physiological deficit, because you don't have much fuel on board or reserves, which is why calorie intake increases, up to as much as 10,000 calories on the 'two marathons a day model', often via six full-on meals a day. These are the ways I move through my everyday life, my training for an ultra endurance event becomes an extension of my everyday life, and the techniques I've personally tried and tested. Yes, there are other factors that come into play at events that are out of my control but if this were not the case, where would the challenge for human potential really be?

On the Three Bare Peaks, I broke a toe on the first day, trying to avoid some people while running down from the summit of Snowdon. I was then faced with running two marathons a day for nine consecutive days and another two mountains to go, barefoot with a broken toe. Other physical challenges included chafing on my inner thighs, which felt as if someone had been at them with sandpaper. It hurt to walk, let alone run. Add to that an upset stomach with D&V, and the last thing I needed was for the family to be let down with our pre-booked family accommodation. But that's what we got – twice. On that run, I looked at what lay ahead over the following nine-day period. Fifty-two miles a day. Despite the uncontrollables, I focused on what I *could* do – with my *breathing and being* coming to the fore. I knew that to be able to endure, I had to do the inner work and deal with the stress and pain. These events are about 'experience, explore and endure', but I have to also enjoy the process. So, my work now became about stripping it back with breathwork, meditation and cold immersion, helping me out of what had the potential to be a victim mindset. And not forgetting that I was a papa and husband.

Day six on the Land's End to John O'Groats run. I've run my 30 miles for the day, interviewed the experts and arrived back at our family accommodation – a converted horsebox – in the Quantock Hills. Arriving there, we find no blankets, no extra clothes or sleeping bags, nothing. So we have to try and figure it out. We wrapped the kids up in as many layers as we could but my daughter Tallulah had the roughest night ever, keeping us up all night. After having no sleep, I had to get up and run another 30 miles. When I arrived back from that day, smashed, I had to interview with Jasmine Hemsley about sustainability. I had to be present, functioning, alert.

Ten miles into day 26, I was forced into the pain cave with an upper ankle sprain. I hobbled on until the pain became unbearable. Until I had to make the even more painful decision to call my support guy James Joyce to rescue me from the side of the road. Picture me there, tears running down my cheeks. We returned to Riddle HQ, where the kids were waiting for Papa to arrive. The beauty of having kids is they just tell it how it is. Lola hit me with, 'You're not going to quit, are you, Papa?' In this cramped mobile home on a Scottish isle, I retreated to the bedroom with my right leg in a bucket of ice and my head in my hands. I went deep into my breath, needing to use my magician skills to imagine myself in a different position. I started to talk to the bear sitting on a log at the back of the pain cave. I knew that the incredibly wise bear would have some important lessons for me, in a time of real adversity. With 120+ miles to go to complete this mission, I couldn't stand up without shearing pain in my ankle and shin. Any advice from the bear was welcome. He said, 'You are in a more powerful position than me, Tony. You can choose to be in the cave or out of the cave, whereas I have to sit back here in the dark on this log. So what's it going to be? Are you going to remain in the back of this dark cave or are you going to step out into the light?'

DEALING WITH PAIN AND DISCOMFORT

We have to create the space for the body to heal itself. To do this I use an up-regulating breathing technique to raise my vibration. You charge the breath with inhales deep into your relaxed belly and then just let the exhale go. Think of a bow and arrow – the drawing back of the bow represents the draw of the inhale, and the release of the arrow represents the exhale – we don't need to push this arrow, the arrow is just released and takes flight. This is about focus, intention and releasing tension, where you are the archer refining each and every release of the arrow.

Play with the number of cycles until things get tingly, then put a breath hold in after one of those arrow-releasing exhales: hold the breath and focus in on the intention. When you do get the urge to inhale, do so gently and slowly.

On day 27 of my 30-day challenge, I emerged from the back of the pain cave with my upper ankle sprain. I was in the process of stripping out anything that wasn't serving the process and ready to leave it. Things were looking a little rough at Riddle HQ. On my blogged stories, you could see the pain and tears on my face. My left ankle was still blown up. As I couldn't hinge at the ankle joint without searing pain, both walking and running were still out of the question. But the bear had thrown me out into the light. Although I had the tools to get me out of this and had been working with breath, mobility and ice, somehow it just wasn't clicking. If this were the last day, no doubt I would have crawled the rest of the run on my hands and knees in the dirt. But it wasn't. It wasn't even the final 30 miles. I had another 120 miles to go – I needed a miracle to continue.

After lots of tossing and turning, I decided to save my hands and knees from the rock, thistle and thorn experience. I took day 27 out to heal myself and rehabilitate and entice both my mind and physiology back out of the pain cave. I had my daughter Lola's voice speaking from the mouth of the cave, 'But you're not going to quit, are you, Papa?' Instead of going out in a blaze of glory and maybe not see this epic journey through, I felt it was much more sustainable to rescue whatever mileage I could over days 28 and 29. Whatever remained would get completed on day 30, even if on my hands and knees. But something shifted within me and I realized what the bear had meant. I had to flip my perception of the situation.

So, on day 27, I flipped my being to healing and moved my perception from the 'Boo hoo, this is all over for poor Tony, just three days to go, and you'll have to quit,' to 'Damn right, Lola, I'm not going to quit, because I'm going to BE healing'. It was the Magician's ability to shift my perception that helped me reappear as the Warrior, tapping into that powerful human potential to not only heal but to go on and complete my mission.

I went on with my upper ankle sprain to complete my mission – with 30 miles on day 28, then two barefoot ultra-marathons: 47 miles on day 29 and 57 miles on the final day. But the perception shifting didn't come without help. I had one of the people who inspire me – plant-based endurance athlete Rich Roll – sending me encouraging messages: 'This is what it's all been about up until now, Tony.' Even messages from others such as 'You can just quit' and 'You don't have to do this' made me realize I could easily slip back into the cave with the bear. I also had a visit from my late grandfather, Charlie Rutter. It was day 29. I'd managed to complete another 30-miler on day 28 and was now out for another day of barefoot shenanigans, when my grandfather popped in for a chat.

My grandfather had a really tough upbringing in Newcastle and knew a thing or two about hardship and going barefoot. His father had died when he was in his teens and he grew up in a gang of kids who ran around with no shoes on, stealing coal from the coal truck to survive. At 15, he made the decision to start walking south with nothing more than a change of underwear in his satchel. He made it to Slough trading estate, where he found work with a decent boss who took him in, bought him his first suit and gave him the money to travel back up to Newcastle and show his family he had work.

Charlie was there on my shoulder, giving me goosebumps and chatting in my ear about hardship, courage, determination, stubbornness and the inner ugly fight – all of the inherited stuff I feel I gained from his proud being. 'Well, you didn't think we were going to make this that easy for you. You were taking the bloody easy route by just running 30 miles a day for 30 days. You know you can access much, much more. We're not going to hand this to you. If you want this, Tony, you're going to have to bloody fight for it.' When he'd finished chewing my ear off in his strong Geordie accent, I looked up and saw the most incredible rainbow and then the sign for the Glenmorangie distillery (Charlie Rutter's whisky). I went on to barefoot-run 47 miles that day and completed my challenge with a gnarly, hilly and rainy 57 miles the day after. Thanks, Grandad, for going through what you had to go through to help me get through what I needed to get through. Bow Rain Riddle was born a month after this event and your rainbow became the inspiration for our son – your great-grandson's – name.

Running barefoot with an upper ankle sprain for 57 miles on the final day of the 879–miles route then planted the seed for me to take on my 'One Man, Two Feet, Three Peaks' challenge, where, one year later at the age of 45, I was attempting to break the men's running record of 9 days 11 hours and 49 minutes. I broke that record by 4 hours and 26 minutes with a time of 9 days 7 hours and 44 minutes.

As a 45-year-old man who was born with club feet, I have to say that running 879 miles barefoot from Land's End to John O'Groats in 30 days, then doing 17 marathons and climbing our three highest mountains barefoot, have to be some pretty awesome highlights of my life thus far.

I am the oldest dude to have completed the route in record time. I am the only father of four to have completed the route in record time. I am the only dude to climb the peaks barefoot and run the roads in barefoot technology in record time. And I am certainly the only dude to have been born with club feet and complete the route in record time.

I did it despite so many variables! But it's testament to my philoso-phy and lifestyle, which have enabled me to go, 'Oh, we *can* do this!' And to get up the next day and do it again, repeating my routines as I do whether on or off an event. I hydrate, I move around, I get underneath the blue sky, then I do some mobility work, then I can run. Then, I look at food again. In the evening, it's exactly the same – as you'll read in the Sleeping and Resting chapter – knocking out all the punishing light and getting back into healing firelight.

Having those practices in place has enabled me to heal, get up and go; to keep restoring. This is intense growth-promoting work. You have the (in this case extreme) stress, you rest, you have the stress, you rest – that promotes growth.

I have a saying, 'trust the process, respect the process, be patient while in the process and when you finally figure out that this is all process, *just be*'.

In BEING, we have to surrender to whatever the process has for us. For me, this came in on day 28, when all I could do was commit to the present and be whatever I needed to be in that moment. This meant, if all my present being was in tune with the healing I needed, then I would heal. But if my whole being was on the fearful 'this could all be over', then the chances were that this epic 900-mile barefoot challenge would have been over well before I saw the completion of day 30. As it turned out, it all became an intense understanding of taking one barefoot step at a time, one breath at a time, to become 100% present in being my human potential. With tears rolling down my cheeks, my message to myself was, 'We are innately wild, connected and empowered beings. Now, go forth and be the awe-inspiring Human you know Nature intended you to be.'

Most of all, I learned that it is WE, and not I, that did all those things. On reflection, it was never about the record. It has and will always be about the journey. And I am certainly not the same man for it.

How can you relate this to your life, your practice?

I am not telling you to carry on running through injury and pain. You may never experience an ultra endurance event. So how does this relate to your life, your experience? Well, sometimes, the odds (whether physical, emotional or practical) might feel stacked against us. I often find that taking things back through one of my down-regulating breathing techniques means I can create a space from the emotional reaction, analyse the situation differently and make an empowered decision. This process allows me to access my human potential and to overcome and grow from each odds-stacking hit of adversity.

Often my most profound lessons have come from the back of the pain cave, in moments of extreme adversity. They have enabled me to hang in there, even when I've been feeling like I'm about to lose my grip on reality. This trusting of the process has enabled me to recognize that everything up until that point has happened for me and will continue to do so. Now, swap out 'me' and insert yourself into the picture . . .

. . . You were born for this. It's in your genes, it's in your DNA, it's the narrative of your evolution to be a resilient being.

What I have learned through my own exploration into finding my self is that you don't have to go down the plant medicine, toad venom-inhaling experiences to find your self. (You can, of course. You might find it enlightening and awakening.) But what I personally learned is that we have all the gear, we just have very little to no idea, and that is where breathing comes in.

Through practices like transformational breath, we can unscrew the intellectual lid and get into those deep emotions and let them out. It doesn't have to be through hallucinatory plant medicine or crystal healing, with animals talking to you, that you suddenly find your voice experience. **We must recognize that the reason we are having to down-regulate is because we are up-regulated.** Just like nature immersion, breathwork can approach the physiological symptoms of stress. A daily 20-minute nature hit will lower heart rate, blood pressure and stress hormones. Ultimately, however, we need to start our recovery at the cause level. I am convinced that, unless we delve deep into the chasms of our internal chaos, we will always be guided by our past events and never reach that authentic being.

Steps to rewilding your breathing and being

 SIT WITH YOURSELF

This is how we check in with our character when no one is there to observe us, where we become the observer of self. It's an opportunity to connect with any of those masks we accumulate over our lifetime. I inherited this practice from my good friend Artur Paulins, an incredibly knowledgeable breathwork coach. Artur's practice involves simply making one hour of meditation a non-effort. It's simple – but not easy.

- Sit down comfortably, close your eyes. Don't do anything, don't even try to control your mind. No focusing on the breath, mantra, a particular thought or emotion, not even exerting effort to stay mindful.
- Just allow the process of being to unravel, allow the space to open up. If you're never alone, how will you ever expect to create the space for your ancestors to come and sit with you and impart their wisdom?

BREATHE FOR A PURPOSE

When setting an intention for the day, it's important to feel the intention in your being. I often use my up-regulating breathing technique (see Dealing with pain and discomfort, page 60) to raise my vibration, then focus in on my intention. If we want to bring around positive change, it's important to remove the negative chatter.

- If my head is busy, I'll box-breathe. Box-breathing involves visualizing a square. You inhale for one side of your imaginary box, hold for the next side, exhale for the next side, hold for the next side and repeat.
- As it's a square, you choose how big you want your square to be. Rather than count the length of the breaths and holds, count the number of squares, up to 20 squares. Then visualize setting your intention free from the centre of your square.

MOVE FROM WORRIER TO WARRIOR

This is a really simple practice that I've introduced to the Riddle kids. You simply exhale the worrier and inhale the warrior.

- Choose a tempo where you can flow from W2W. Rather like drawing a circle, with half the circle representing the inhale, the other the exhale, with no breaks. In with the warrior – out with the worrier – in with the warrior – out with the worrier.

- Repeat, repeat, repeat until you feel it in your being – and then, out loud, say, 'I am an innately wild, connected and empowered being!'

REWILD AT HEART

We can often get lost in our heads; our minds and our logical brains trying to run the show. Personally, I've found that to discover a better sense of being, I have to reconnect with my heart, to rewild it. This is about developing an emotional awareness and preparedness, and finding absolute balance of the outside in and the inside out. The practice is really quite simple. Get out of your head and tune into your heart.

- Place your hand on your heart: feel it, tune into the rhythm, the rhythm of you and your being. Now relax your face, your jaw and your belly. Choose a word to represent each beat. I like to keep it simple by adding 'love' to every thump of my chest and being love. You can choose whatever powerful words you want to pump through you.
- Choose long, slow cycles of breath, minimizing the drop off and pick up of the breath and keep bringing your attention back to the heart. You Are Loved!

ROAR LIKE A BEAST

Sometimes deep conversations aren't profound enough, nor is deep breathwork or meditation. To avoid emotional stagnation manifesting into something destructive, it is important to release our tensions, frustrations, worries, fears and overwhelming emotions out into the world. The practice of a good primal roar into the pillow of love has been profound for my sanity. We often discuss how important it is for us men to show vulnerability, to share how we're feeling and express our emotions. With men being three times more likely to die by suicide than women, this has never been more evident. I feel it's equally important for us to shout, roar and let all that vulnerability out, but in a place where we are not terrifying the divine feminine. This is one powerful release that will enhance those other inner practices, getting right into the belly of the beast.

- Take an exhale to create the space for a deep belly breath, then let the beast out of the cage. Roar, shout, scream – whatever needs to get out, let it go, let it out, be that into the woods or in the pillow or in the car.
- This is your permission to lose your shit into the pillow; every part of your life will benefit from this emotional explosion. Five rounds should do you.

BREATHE FOR SLEEPING

When you want to get to sleep, the last thing you want to be doing is thinking. Here's a technique where you focus on your breathing, then get into a count.

- If you place your finger on your pulse, you'll find that when you inhale, your pulse will pick up; when you exhale, your pulse will lower. Inhale through the nose, but this time extend the exhale. Think of the exhale being one third longer than the inhale, but also allow the breath to flow without pushing. As you exhale, imagine you are softening, as if with each exhale your tissue is literally melting off your bones.

- Don't count. For a longer breath session, where the object-ive is to find stillness, it's best to think less to tune in more. Try not to dwell on counting when letting out the breath. Just let it go and take it back to the intention of the extended, melting exhales, softening into your bed.

BREATHE TO DIGEST

The best practice I've found for digestion is so soft and subtle that it often appears we're not breathing at all. Think of a pulse on a heart-rate monitor with its convex and concave waves and how this represents the breath: the convex representing the inhale and the concave representing the exhale. With this practice, try and transform the convex wave of the inhale and concave wave of the exhale from waves into almost unrecog-nizable ripples.

- If you hold your hand underneath your nose, try to minim-ize your ripples, so that you can barely distinguish between your inhale and exhale.
- You'll find your palms becoming quite sweaty and your salivary enzymes kicking in. Welcome to your parasympa-thetic rest-and-digest state – a state where you are primed for digestion.

BECOME YOUR GRATITUDE

One of my old friends, Mark Rumbles, told me how his kids had seen a video of me immersing in a cold lake and had ever since been randomly shouting out, 'I AM GRATEFUL'. This is a powerful, contagious and immensely rewarding process. To begin with, you might feel a little awkward but if you keep going, it will become you.

- Say it loud, say it proud, feel it in your heart and become gratitude.
- I started this practice at the lake at 42 Acres in Somerset. I'd drop into the 'I am nature' state, with 100 cycles of alternate nostril breaths, then immerse in the cold waters of the some-times frozen lake. I'd then stand upon the banks of the lake roaring, 'I AM GRATEFUL', with my hands reaching up and out to the universe. Then I'd bring my hands in to beat my chest with a strong 'YEAH'. I'd reset this three times.

NEXT » MOVING AND PLAYING

- Meet Yehudi and learn how an 80-year-old man learned to move properly and overcome eight decades of birth trauma.
- Learn how to rewild your running style.
- Find out if you're ready to re-child.

CHAPTER 5

Moving and Playing

Yehudi wakes in his air-purified bedroom by the light of the morning sun. Before jumping from his bed, he pandiculates like a cat – stretching out with his arms and legs, circling his wrists and ankles to fire up his neural pathways. After doing all the usual things we human animals need to do when we first wake, he wanders down to the next floor of his house where he has strung up a set of gymnastic rings from the door to his home office. Yehudi tightens his hand grip around the rings and hangs with his body weight for a minute before entering the office. He has made room in his office for a matted area for mobility work. So, he proceeds to get down on to the floor and run through a flow to mobilize his hips and enable him to check in with his posture. He then sits in a resting position on the ground, meditates for a few minutes and checks in with himself before turning on his computer and checking his inbox. His desk is no longer like any ordinary desk, because, despite his 80 years of age, Yehudi could easily justify a squishy armchair. Instead, Yehudi has a standing desk. Underneath it, he keeps different-sized stones on which he stands to enable his feet to become compliant. With this set-up, he is forced to keep shape-shifting – moving his body from his toes up to stay upright – never stagnating, always uploading brain-nourishing sensory information.

Humans are the ultimate adaptors. For good or bad, we will always adjust to the norms our environment presents us with. Most of us have simply adapted to become the sedentary, fearful, tentative modern humans our environments are facilitating, without considering whether there is another way. Yet, at the core of our being, we remain natural animals, primed for the wild. Our bodies, brains and hormones are set to the tune of the natural environment we were once so at one with. As movement should be an opportunity to unravel that normalized structure, we're going to explore how you can get back to a playful state that can help you in your daily living. First, let's look at how we've made moving and playing more difficult for ourselves than it needs to be.

Like all animals, we possess primordial blueprints which we download from our evolutionary database. These blueprints are our hardwiring, our innate index that nature has bestowed on us to promote a life of nourishment, fulfilment and happiness. This biological directory has taken millions of years to become established. In our evolutionary past, movement is life. Now, we view movement through such a domesticated lens. We have forgotten and become disconnected from the vaults of this incredible and immense natural database, which enables us to be *remarkable* in the ways we move our bodies.

Before we are born, we already have trillions of individual cells moving and working in perfect unison, months before our lungs even catch oxygen. So far, so good. Once born, we naturally want to stretch, touch, flail, move, roll, crawl and explore. Movement is the foundation of our development, our learning, our very existence. Yet, in modern life, it all starts to go pear-shaped. Sooner or later, we're put into that baby car seat, which begins to shape us into another human with a C-shaped spine, one that's inappropriately aligned with being an upright biped.

By the time we've reached the intellectual developmental stage, often around the time we start school, we're trained to move less and less, so as to conform to social norms that revolve around conforming, behaving, sitting still and staying quiet. At school, we learn domesticated behaviour and are moulded into fine examples of what our modern tribe expects us to become: socially compliant. We are ordered not to run in the corridors, to sit quietly on chairs in a room full of other children of the same age. We see each member of our new tribe sitting down, including the teacher, who takes the position of tribal elder. But sitting for long periods works at odds with the symbiotic relationship between our minds and bodies that we need to thrive. The result is stagnation and restriction. Our cells move into the state of protection and switch their focus to survival and *away from* growth. I honestly believe it's quite traumatizing to take a playful child, put them in a chair and refuse them movement for hours on end every day.

As supposed relief from daily sitting, children are regularly and routinely released to venture outside on to a concrete surface, for 'playtime'. This is usually our first exposure to the idea of exercise. In reality, it's anything but free movement and spontaneous play. We're having to fit our movement into a set time frame, which over time reduces to just an hour or two of 'Physical Education' each week. Here we are probably encouraged to take up specialist sports for an expression of our physicality, in substitute for our natural play. These sports – football, netball, cross country – will teach the body to move repetitively in inefficient ways and usually only for set periods of time. This is our first introduction to exercise vs movement in the Human Zoo.

Not all kids can be specialists but we are all generalists. There's a difference between a generalist mover and a specialist mover. At one stage, we could all forage, move through a landscape, walk, run, climb, balance – whatever we needed to do. But owing to the sedentary lives and the environments we inhabit – which discourage play and free movement outside the confines of a gym – most of us simply do not understand quite how amazing we actually are when it comes to our *capacity to move*. At our very core we are generalist movers. We weren't designed for restrictive, repetitive, single-plane actions.

Being exercised out of this naturally playful state continues as we grow into our teens and early adulthood. I call it the linear approach to exercise. Squat thrusts, burpees, push-ups. Sets and reps. Just pushing and pulling movements, when we have this incredible capacity to move. It's all an insult to the evolutionary model of what we can actually achieve with our physicality.

A quick look at our ancestry will lend us clues of how we can return to a life of nourishment, fulfilment and happiness. In his book *Born to Run*, Christopher McDougall finds that before sports came along, running was a form of play. He writes, 'We made it into a competition, whereas that competition doesn't exist in nature. Running is for survival. But there are tribes like the Mexican Tarahumara who have taken running beyond that. It's a playful thing for them, a spiritual process, not an exercise. Their play state is found through running as a tribe.'

Yes, that's right, inside each and every one of us resides a bounding, jumping, barefoot-running, tree-climbing, body-popping, cliff-diving superhuman capable of incredible feats of movement. You are innately capable of being just as jaw-dropping a mover as the latest Ninja Warrior champion – isn't that incredible? It's in our genes, it's in our DNA, it's the narrative of our evolution.

Moving

Yehudi ventures down to the kitchen where he whizzes up a super-smoothie to take to his office. His daily smoothie is packed full of pro-, pre- and symbiotic foods, like yoghurt, leafy greens, avocados, seeds, walnuts and berries – everything his cells and bacteria need to thrive. He then hops into his shower, to which he's attached a water-purifying filter that removes chlorine. He steps into his suit and his Vivobarefoot shoes, which enable his feet to behave how nature intended them to. He kisses his wife goodbye, grabs his super-smoothie and takes a 10-minute walk to the Tube station. As Yehudi is now a biologically normal 80-year-old, he politely declines the other passengers' offers of their seats. Instead of sitting, he opts to raise the eyebrows of his train mates by hanging from the overhead handrail. While the train is moving, Yehudi grips tightly and keeps his body weight hanging, only resting his feet on the floor when the train reaches each station stop, until he hits his destination.

We have an amazing range of movement – when we take the opportunity to develop it. We can walk, run, sprint, jump, balance, climb, swim, lift, hang, carry, throw, catch, kick and dance, and let's not forget all of the postural challenges required of the multi-tasking, multi-shape-making hunter-gatherer who negotiates an unpredictable wild landscape.

On top of this, we are also in possession of something quite unique in the animal kingdom. We have the amazing ability to impersonate any animal that has ever existed, in addition to being able to push and explore the abilities of our own unique human bodies through movement and play.

Now, doesn't that make the treadmill seem dull?

But Yehudi hasn't always been this way. For 70+ years he was told (and believed) that he couldn't move, wasn't strong or capable, that his body was broken. He made a commitment for his 50th wedding anniversary to climb Mount Everest and arrived at my studio on a mission to relearn how to walk the way nature always intended him to. Born with the ability to walk naturally, Yehudi was ready to relearn from the ground up. So, as with all of my clients, we began on the floor. Relearning required much humility and vulnerability from Yehudi as we went right back to the beginning; progressing from various ground-resting positions to develop a strong superstructure. Correct ground sitting then enabled the easy moving from one posture to another without the use of hands, creating foundational movement patterns on which to build Yehudi's new stance. We progressed to basic crawling, then more complex crawls to reconnect neurological and physiological pathways. Once Yehudi was walking upright, strong and in possession of a rewilded pair of feet, we rediscovered the ancient practice of hanging. This was a huge game changer – lifting up Yehudi's ribcage, strengthening his mid back and connecting him with his wild 76-year-old posture. Building on his first experience of rewilding, Yehudi eventually achieved his dream of making it to Everest Base Camp.

Ask yourself, are the movements you are making serving you? Are you the best physical representation of yourself? Are you moving in ways which nourish your brain before nourishing your need for an Instagram-worthy physique? If the answer to these questions is not an honest and confident 'yes!', then I'm here to help show you exactly how to reset your templates so that you can become a master of your environment, a master of your cells, of your movement and of your self, just like Yehudi has done.

We have become so reliant on the idea that our movement must be accessed within designated time periods and called 'exercise'. So, an integral part of rewilding your movement is altering your perception of exercise. We are born with the inherent knowledge of how to move and play. You don't need a Pilates or Alexander Technique practitioner to teach you how to stand up and walk at the age of one, so why would you as you grow into an adult?

There's a world of change waiting for you.

Movement is happiness

Movement is the place most of my clients begin their own lifestyle evolutions. Being able to move well and freely directly impacts your level of wellbeing and happiness – it's that big a deal!

It's not enough just to 'think happy'. When your body is starved of movement, your joints aren't working well, your inner systems are stagnant and your muscles are tense or in pain. Think of your body as a fleshy vessel for your mind: the more quality, natural movement you feed it, the easier it is to feel relaxed mentally.

The journey towards better movement begins by helping people reground themselves with foot protocols and ground sitting positions. We rewild their feet and their footwear and reconnect to the ground with the same ground sitting protocols as Yehudi implemented, the same ones which form the daily movement practices of traditional cultures.

First, reground yourself

The first part of regrounding yourself is empowering your feet. Once you commit to reconnecting to your feet, you'll be amazed where they will take you.

Let's take a look at the human foot for a moment.

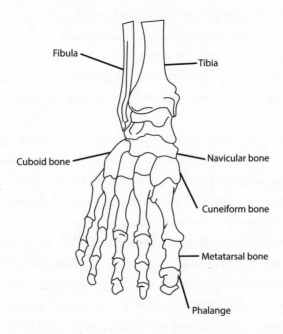

Each foot is made up of 26 bones (so for both feet that's a quarter of all of the bones in the body), and a combined 100 muscles, tendons and ligaments, which are capable of providing a super-strong foundation.

Think of the most sophisticated suspension system, maybe that of the Range Rover, and you are still not even close to the profoundly advanced and complex sensory system you own within your humble feet. We have the ability to mould, grip, grab and switch from compliance and softness to tension and stiffness in a millisecond. Information about our terrain is gathered by 200,000 nerve receptors in our feet and used to soften or stiffen our feet and joints, and to alter our posture as a protection mechanism against injury as we move.

As a survival mechanism, our movement brain makes subtle micro adjustments to the shapes we make over varying surfaces. This not only minimizes the risk of injury, it maximizes the efficiency of our movement. All this enables us to shape-shift in the blink of an eye. So, if your feet are natural foot-shaped and you understand their role as the base of your bio-superstructure and the feeder of your bio-shape, so will all your joint actions. So, in turn, will all the complexities of your muscular and tendon system.

The reason I place such importance on foot health is because our feet are our ultimate foundation; the place from which all other movement and positioning comes. Naturally wide, bare feet offer strong yet flexible foundations upon which to build extraordinary shapes and movements. Yes, you might be able to walk, run, sprint, jump, balance, climb, swim, lift, carry, throw, catch, kick and dance. However, unless you are performing these actions with a foundation of proper, natural movement – meaning all of your muscles, tendons, ligaments, bones and joints are in harmony – you are setting yourself up for inevitable health problems later down the line.

In 2019 Dr Kris D'Aout, Senior Lecturer in Musculoskeletal Biology at the University of Liverpool, together with a PhD student, conducted a phenomenal piece of research where they measured the increase in foot strength wearing Vivobarefoot shoes, showing that there was a 60% improvement in foot strength after just six months of reconnecting to the function of their feet through wearing barefoot shoes.

In another study, titled 'Preventing falls in older people by an innovative connected shoe: development and biomechanics study', D'Aout discovered that balance in Vivobarefoot shoes is improved by up to 40% compared to regular padded shoes. Both these studies should leave us questioning where all the scientific research and innovations of billion-dollar aesthetic/athletic shoe brands has got us, if, by going back to foot-shaped shoes with as little protection as possible, feet get stronger, and balance and mobility improves.

D'Aout said: 'Our study adds to the increasing body of evidence that for many people, less (shoe) is more. A minimal shoe helps our feet to be used how they are supposed to. I believe that footwear design should be evidence-based rather than just aesthetical. Our feet are our only point of contact with the environment, so having the right shoe for the right foot is crucial.'

From a parenting perspective the most important take-home from these studies is that grown-ups need to transition and adapt to get their foot strength and ability back. So as grown-ups, if we are to improve foot strength by 60% and balance by 40% by returning feet to a naturally functioning footwear, we have to have a pretty solid reason as to why we would place natural feet in such unnatural footwear in the first place . . . by wearing compromising footwear we lose 60% of foot strength and 40% of our balance. Imagine raising a whole generation of kids whose feet don't need fixing. Remember, kids don't need rebooting, reconnecting, rewilding and empowering, they just need us to create environments that enable their wild innate abilities to thrive, and the shoe is an environment for the foot, is it not?

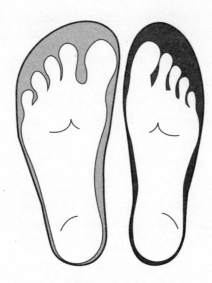

Left: A healthy foot with space; Right: a typical modern shoe which restricts foot mobility

TOEGA

Healthy toes are vital for healthy feet, which are vital for healthy, natural movement. I have devised a series of 'Toega' exercises (yoga for your feet) to transform your feet from zoo shoe-shaped to natural feet-shaped. Rewilded feet are wide in the toe pads, providing a stable platform for movements including standing, squatting, lifting, balancing, jumping, walking and running.

First you have to take the time to reconnect with those feet. Take it from a man who knows; I was born with a deformity in my feet, where I had to wear plaster-cast boots and braces to return my feet to the 'perceived' alignment of how feet should be.

To start rewilding your feet you need to reconnect to them. Take a moment to pause and feel through the bare pads of your feet. There are thousands of exteroceptors in the soles of your feet, equal to your wild hands, and they can often become desensitized by cushioned footwear and linear surfaces.

Each of these Toega exercises will reboot the connection with your toes being your body's natural anchor, lever and pivot. Perform these daily to improve mobility, flexibility and strength in the feet, big toe and ankles. Do them twice a day if possible and give yourself 3–4 minutes to complete the exercises – the longer, the better.

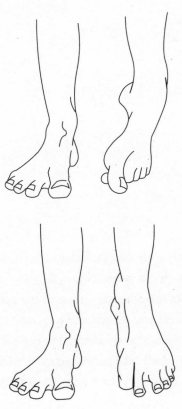

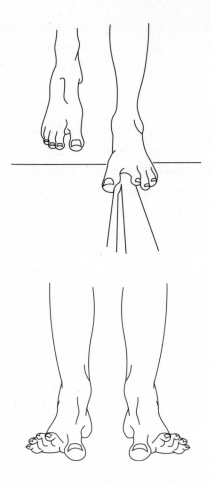

- Stand with your head, chest and pelvis stacked above your base of support (your two wild feet), soften your knees. With your eyes closed, tune into the pads of your feet: the spaces where you recognize your body weight.
- Scan the soles of your feet and notice all the areas that connect to the earth: the pads of your feet. The way your weight is spread between your big toe, your little toe and the heels.

- With your weight evenly balanced over these three points, two-thirds of your body weight is organized in the front of your feet, and one third balanced in your heels.
- And now, using the illustrations, I want you to play with your animal pads.

Then, get back to your regular practices

Having returned to the simplicity of groundwork, people find they miraculously seem to enjoy their original movement systems of choice in a much more efficient, injury-free, honest way. This applies to running, yoga, martial arts, walking 10,000 steps per day – whatever it is they were doing before.

REWILD YOUR RUNNING STYLE

Running is a macro skill and one of our primary locomotive patterns. However, to be a skilled runner you have to run as naturally as possible, otherwise you lose touch with your innate efficiency and risk falling into a constant cycle of injury. Skilful natural running is focused on three things:

- Posture (wild upright posture – head and chest over hips)
- Rhythm (wild elastic efficiency – quick cadence – around 180 steps per minute)
- Relaxation (wild connection – nasal breathing techniques to tune you into your mindful practice to aid efficiency and recovery)

You're going to be playing with reconnecting your wild form with the wild functions of rhythm and relaxation. Rather than see running as something you have to endure, I want you to access your playful state of mind. Think 'flow'. Don't push; pull instead. Lift your head and chest up to look at the horizon, not down at the pavement. Lead with your heart, let your feet follow and keep this mantra in mind to maintain that lovely, wild, upright form. Inhale through the nose for a tempo of four micro breaths and exhale for a tempo of four micro breaths. Allow your breath to dictate your pace. If you push too hard, you'll feel the need to mouth breathe. Slow things up and take it back to the nasal breath.

Lose your Western sedentary stoop

When we spend too much of our lives sitting in chairs or on sofas, we actually compromise all of the areas that should be providing movement and dumb down the areas that should be playing a role in stabilization by building those fundamental foundations to our superstructure. Just imagine all of the amazing physiological potential we are missing out on from having adopted our single Western 'typing and swiping' position.

Ground rest positions – from kneeling through to squatting – are human milestones of development, and it's never too late to learn and redevelop. These are the fundamental foundations, before walking, balancing, jumping, running, crawling and climbing and all other movement skills that the successful wild urbanite can access.

Forget learning to run before you can walk. Without honouring a ground practice, we're all learning to walk, run, balance, jump, lift or climb before we have even learned to stand correctly.

The Hadza tribe from Tanzania (see page 132) sit for 10 hours, just like our sedentary selves. However, their sitting is based around ground-resting positions that keep nourishing their mobility and strength – in order to feed their incredible physiology and capacity to move and play, both efficiently and effectively.

Squatting, for instance, is a rest position in nature that allows us to maintain the same body weight through the soles of our feet to the earth comparable to when we stand on two feet. It nourishes the appropriate joint actions and posture needed to be an upright endurance animal. Whereas sitting in a chair is counter to how our posture and our joints naturally want to behave, or where we store our body weight. Squatting supports standing much better than sitting is able to. In terms of our need to be effective when we're on our two feet, the gap between sitting and standing is much more difficult for us to cope with.

I see the squat as a fundamental foundation to my own barefoot endurance athleticism, but my squat isn't 'exercise', it is a playful rest position of subconscious choice, which I now choose over sitting in a chair. Chair sitting has now become uncomfortable for me and, because of my hardwired 'am I going to get injured?' mindset, is too alarming to want to spend too long in the Western sedentary stoop. It would also be the saboteur of my endurance athletic feats – leading me to need more symptom relief rehab. If someone asks how I run for 10–12 hours a day for a number of consecutive days, I start with the explanation that I spend 10–12 hours connecting to the ground and not the chair – be it squatting or standing.

Playing

play /pleɪ
Verb: to engage in activity for enjoyment and recreation rather than a serious or practical purpose.

When I speak of play, I am not referring to the intellectual states of play we access through board games, competitive sports or Candy Crush. On the contrary, the kind of restorative play we innately need is a multi-sensory, explorative, boundless, creative feast that nourishes our physical, emotional and imaginative worlds. It expands consciousness and stretches time. So I'm talking about our need to rewild play, which means tapping into 'Play State' and finding your 'Play Personality'.

Free flow

The positive psychologist Mihaly Csikszentmihalyi was the first to identify and research the concept of flow, in 1990. A Flow State is recognized as a mental state in which a person is fully absorbed in and focused on an activity to the extent that they lose sense of time and space. As a result, the concept of Flow has been adopted by busy, entrepreneurial Westerners and popularized as a 'productivity hack'. Play State is really just Flow State. But here's the good news: we don't need to consciously create time and space and focus to get into play state, because it should come naturally as a result of being nurtured during childhood developmental years.

When you see no difference between play and work, you are in perpetual play state. Due to their perpetual play state, most hunter-gatherer populations do not possess a word for 'work'. Instead, their childhood playtime merges naturally into productive play as adults. Their children transition seamlessly from play hunting and gathering, preparing dinner, building shelters, warding off predators, pretend parenting, maintaining communal peace, into one day doing these tasks for real, without ever having left their play state.

The act of play also prompts movement for no goal other than movement itself, which physically processes the energies that we hold on to in our bodies, thus shifting them. Even in tribal adulthood today, dance ceremonies and rituals survive to allow that hunter-gatherer ability to enter smoothly into a state of flow and release trauma through play. That is what rites of passage and ceremony are about at their core – getting deep into our reptilian brains to stir up our traumas and release them through the play state.

The huge difference in the play process today is that, because our kids aren't spending enough time in nature, it's hard for them to connect with or imagine they are part of any overarching system. So where tribal youngsters can become the plants, the rocks, the animals, children in the Human Laboratory are now becoming the car, the parent with their face in their screen, the streets littered with Starbucks takeaway cups. It's little wonder we have escalating environmental, connective, creative, imaginative and mental health issues in children as they develop.

When you bring play into movement the possibilities for fun, and for brain growth opportunities, really are boundless. We have the chance to remind our human tribes how we were born to play. When we re-child and reintroduce play, both by ourselves and with our kids, in these biologically normal ways, we are lessening the effects of play amnesia on the next generations.

The purpose of play

Play serves so many purposes in our development and sense of discovery and wonder. You only have to take a look at the animal kingdom to find evidence of the importance of play; play behaviour is displayed by almost all the animal kingdom, showing it is vital for survival. Dr Stuart Brown, founder of the National Institute of Play, finds that play enables us to 'open ourselves to discovery, possibility and creativity . . . It is the most significant factor in determining our success and happiness.' He says:

'As a scientist I know that a behaviour this pervasive throughout human culture and across the evolutionary spectrum most likely has a survival value. Otherwise, it would have been eliminated through natural selection . . .

'You see, animals simply don't partake in uneconomical behaviours. Why would skilled species – species which possess remarkable physical adaptations for survival in hostile conditions – use valuable, survival-dependent time and energy in apparently unproductive activity like play?

'It was upon learning that mountain goats literally risk death to satisfy their need to play, despite the lethal dangers directly involved in running around with one another on sheer cliff faces, where one extra zealous wrestle means certain death, that the significance of play was solidified for me.'

Play serves an essential function in the development of healthy, happy humans and functioning societies. I can't help but feel we have been missing something fundamental when it comes to an additional purpose of play. How could it be that evolution would allow us to carry trauma around with us in the long term – a sore knee, the grief from a grandparent's death, hearing our parents shouting at one another, the way so many of us do? Surely, with nature being as intelligent as we know she is, in play she has provided us with a mechanism to process traumatic experiences, instead of holding on to them and going about our lives as they fester and grow inside us, causing all manner of issues. What if we began to see play as a key tool in healing our past disconnection and trauma?

KNEE BONE ATTACHED TO THE . . .

I was holding a workshop at a festival. Halfway through a few warm-ups, with playful head-to-head movement and mirroring patterns, where the participants can be found in pure animalistic flow, a remarkable example of the incredible way in which play state can process trauma walked right up to me.

Mid-flow, one of the yogis came over, looking slightly awestruck, and said, 'I don't understand it, my knee has stopped hurting!' She went on to explain how she'd been plagued by a knee problem for years. Yet since she had begun the play session less than an hour before, the pain had gone.

In response, I placed my hands on her head and proclaimed, 'Praise the Lord, you are healed!' (No, I didn't, only playing with you . . .)

The miracle here is entirely attributable to our human biology. What had actually happened was that this particular yogi had become so absorbed in the moment, so deep into her play state, that she had imagined herself as something and someone else. Through her playful capacity to move, she had stepped outside the injured yogi and had become a cat, a monkey, a hand-balancing circus performer. She had overridden the protective mechanism of pain that had been inhibiting her knee from going into important, nourishing and healing ranges of movement. She had processed the physical trauma of her injury.

Don't get me wrong, I am not suggesting play in itself can heal acute physical injury. But due to the declining means of trauma release within the modern lifestyle, the pain that once protected this woman's knee had long outstayed its welcome in her body and had begun doing more harm than good. Her body had been thrust into and held in protection mode, trying to protect an injury which no longer needed protecting.

Childhood traumatic experiences are part of the freeze mechanism of stress, where our brain and body are frozen in an anticipatory stress response. This long-term suppression-freeze response leads to excess energy being trapped in our bodies and can result in chronic physical, mental and emotional distress, or the negativity brain bias loop.

Robert Sapolsky is a neuroendocrinology researcher, author and professor of biology, neurology and neurological sciences at Stanford University. In his book *Why Zebras Don't Get Ulcers* he notes how many animals post-threat will process the trauma of their life-threatening attack by shaking and tremoring, known as neurogenic tremors. As with the rest of the animal kingdom, we too have the ability to shake off our post-threat traumas. BUT where the animal kingdom can still access nature's way of processing acute stress by shaking it off and getting themselves back to living in the moment, humans have become disconnected from this natural response of nervous system recalibration. This means our emotions go unprocessed and are frozen in the moment.

Long-term suppression leads to excess energy being trapped in our bodies. This results in chronic emotional and physical tension and mental distress. You can address some of this with the Shake to unbreak exercises at the end of this chapter (page 117).

Born to play

Our play state, our innate need to play as part of the animal kingdom, is nature's way of getting us to dismantle or deconstruct our physical and emotional traumas. Play is nature's way of unravelling trauma – an inbuilt, immensely powerful tool for removing the biologically detrimental effects of unprocessed trauma. How traumatizing would that be, then, to remove it at such an early age in that school environment? Why would we inhibit something so valued?

While many experts claim play exists to facilitate education – and I do not disagree with this – I believe its purpose in nature goes far deeper, right into our reptilian and mammalian brains. Through play, we can imagine ourselves in different situations and find creative solutions to avoid becoming stuck in the trauma cycle. We can also put ourselves in the place of others, thus nurturing our capacity for compassion, empathy and forgiveness. I like to think of this phenomenon as 'play plasticity': when our brains are being constantly rewired through play state, we are able to step aside and sense ourselves in a more favourable position and have the confidence and creativity to get there in reality.

As little children, when our ability to communicate verbally is limited, we cannot go to our parents and fully express our emotions. As adults in our contemporary world, where play is anything but play, we store away our unexpressed emotions and go about our lives carrying their weight with us, as 'baggage'. Yet nature has equipped us with the capacity to play them out and release them that way. It's an alternative means of therapy without us being aware that we're doing anything other than having fun.

You need only observe children allowed to explore their own capacity to turn anything into playtime and you can see at its very essence that play is *intrinsic*. There's something primal about the collective emotions roused through playful human contact and connection with our creativity. Absorbed in play state and using their imaginations, children develop entire worlds together, weaving effortlessly in and out of mental and physical realities, soaking up and having fun with everything there is to learn around them.

What can you take from this concept of free play? Let's break it down . . .

- Free play deconstructs the concept of hierarchy between children and adults because it is not directed by the parents.
- Children are able to feel in control of their own time and how they use it, which is why they will often even play at being the parents.
- Similarly, free play obliterates the divide between class systems, race – even between species.
- Play is non-discriminate; everybody can play together and anybody can be anybody or anything else during play.
- By visiting birth, death, marriage and the nuances of family dynamics within these creatively constructed worlds, children come to understand rites of passage; they resolve differences and vent frustrations; they explore the unbound possibilities of their own inner worlds and those of their tribe.
- Subsequently, free-playing children learn the boundaries of their external kingdom and their roles within it by fully immersing in interdependence.

Through play, children discover their uniqueness. They are able to explore outside the confines of their ego, or self, as they experiment with being anything and anyone that their imagination can dream up. When in their natural state, they are entirely eco, at one with nature.

What of adults? As with movement, we too are attracted to the sense of unbound freedom and dynamic exhilaration that play can bring. Sometimes we are drawn to that lingering memory of satisfied excitement that playtime gifts us. Yet we resist that pull. Every time we do hit the replay button, though, we rekindle a part of our play state and edge a little closer to that innate, child-like happiness.

The trouble is, it's hard work being an adult. When did life get so serious?! Anyone can get stuck and many of us will experience periods of depression or points of stagnation in our lives. During these times, we struggle to see a way through or imagine ourselves in a better position. You might have lost the ability to visualize a positive future.

Moving and playing call us back to our primordial hardwiring, but we view them through such a domesticated lens that we have become disconnected from this incredible natural database, one which enables us to be simply awe-inspiring in the ways in which we move our bodies and flex our imaginations.

We've effectively eliminated free play from our modern lives and, in doing so, have switched off our biological filter for processing life's experiences and trauma – which is why we're all so unnaturally weighed down by it. We have cut off our inbuilt filter for pain, distress, sadness, grief, anger, rejection, hurt and fear and so have no option but to store all of these emotions in our bodies.

To set this thrill-seeking, natural mover within us free, we need to access the right tribe of influence and rewild our movement through play. Through play, we can bring our imaginations back to life. When we can picture ourselves somewhere better, we can manifest a positive future. The good news is that it is never too late to find your movement flow, uncover and hone your own hidden movement skills and talents, reconnect with the body nature intended you to have and astound yourself with what your body and imagination can do. All it takes is the right knowledge and the flipping of the ignition switch to a new, awesome YOU.

It's time to *re-child*

Rewilded play teaches children unbounded life skills and nourishes them at a biological level, fulfilling so many of their fundamental needs. Fortunately, the gap between socially normal and biologically normal begins to close with each generation of rewilded kids who have adopted a new norm – which is where you come in. You can help close the gap. By making the choice to rewild your own play, you can be the change and set a new example, making a radical difference to the collective health and happiness of future generations. Have you ever had a better excuse to have fun? When it comes to rewilding play for adults, surely we have to rename it 're-childing'?

'I have waited my whole life for this!' yells journalist Eminé Rushton, while rough-and-tumbling with a group of other giggling grown-ups in the dewy morning grass. Like you and me, Eminé was born into this life primed for play. But, somewhere along the line of modern conditioning, she lost her connection to it. Reconnecting with what is often perceived as inappropriate behaviour for a respectable adult can be a powerful tool towards transformative healing.

'My retreat with Tony Riddle and several of his hand-picked and trusted healing practitioners changed my life. I say that without the least bit of hyperbole – this is the truth. Even as I arrived, I had no idea what Tony was capable of – of resetting our bodies and returning our minds to their natural, resting, thriving, crystal-clear state. Years of petty hurts and pain peeled away, I revisited the real meaning of movement and got better acquainted with my body's own remarkable strength, mobility and intuitive responses . . . I tapped into so many parts of me that I'd never even been introduced to before. That Tony so wholly and passionately walks his talk is the real key here – you're not witnessing marketing spiel, you're witnessing a living, breathing, thriving example of unsullied human nature. It should be the norm, but given how far removed we are from our nature – it's become extraordinary. His message, "what is socially normal is biologically abnormal", really stayed with me . . . as did so many other lessons during those four days, all of which have radically changed my life.'

Eminé Rushton

It's a couple of months after the life-changing retreat I held for journalists, where I first met Eminé. I'm back at 42 Acres, this time hosting a weekend for another group. After an immersion in re-wilding, Eminé is on the ground, barefoot, hugging, laughing uncontrollably, wrapping her arms and legs around people who were relative strangers just yesterday. This is re-childing at its very best.

Are you ready to be hit with the recognition of just how wondrous you are as a human being? I trust, by now, that you're not seeing this as moving well for physical or sporting prowess, or any of the linear exercise stuff. What I'm suggesting has its benefits for all forms of how we move, going back to moving through a landscape that's forever changing, all undulating surfaces. I'm talking about how we can rewire the brain through sensory pathways.

My work is about using sensory experience to help wire and rewire the brain, whoever we are. People can be very awkward when they first come to a workshop. It's as if they're still riding on the Tube and don't want to have eye or body contact. Yet, 20 minutes in, they're rolling around on the floor, wrestling and licking each other's cheeks. So quickly we're unravelling and deconstructing that process of awkward adulthood and experiencing trauma release.

The act of play can literally fast-track us to a state of meditative expression. It is in this creative, joyous state that we can suspend the intellectual mind and tap into the wondrous, infinite realms of imagination and collective consciousness. When we are 'exercising', we're often looking at the clock, waiting for the hour session to finish. In the workshops and activities I run, I notice that people get completely immersed, with no concept of time. Here, we rediscover a sanctuary free from judgement, fear – even pain – and the negative language and emotions that have come to cripple us in adulthood. Play, in essence, is rewilding. It is an opportunity to redefine and recreate the adult mind by rewilding our innermost child.

To quote Dr Brown, the scientist that I mentioned earlier, 'In an ideal world the work play differential would cease to exist . . . I would encourage people to approach life as an integrative process.

Incorporating play seamlessly into their daily activities – and this includes work.'

Just take a moment to picture the incredible, life-changing impact that relearning how to do that would have on your everyday life and the lives of those around you. What if your nine-to-five, the weekly shop, going to the tip, the daily commute could become . . . fun? Just as through breath we have the power to change our brain chemistry, alter our mood, enter profound blissful states of wellbeing, reach Nirvana and immerse ourselves calmly into ice baths, the same states can occur through play and even through work, if we can learn from our primal ancestors and start to alter our perception and how to consider work as play.

Are you ready for a natural high?

Through the wonder that is evolution, you are in possession of the most incredible inner cocktail shaker filled with happy-making neurochemicals that you can alchemize and set back to work for you, through simple play states. You will likely already be familiar with some of these neurochemicals, especially if you are a runner. Even if you have never heard of endorphins, you'll know all about how they make you feel as the chemical responsible for blessing you with that coveted 'runners' high'.

If you enjoy a good hug, you will be acquainted with oxytocin, the chemical that makes you feel warm, happy and safe when someone gives you a squeeze. People call oxytocin the touch hormone. So we shouldn't be surprised that psychologists are starting to talk about 'touch hunger'.

If you are an ardent typer and swiper, you will have felt the effects of dopamine every time your phone notifies you that you have a new like or follower. We understand it as a seeking hormone or motivational molecule. Have an orgasm and you've got dopamine at 100%. When kids are caught up in gaming, they experience a dopamine hit of between 100 and 400%. (And you wonder why you can't drag them away.) There's no need for them to go seeking pleasure as they grow up – they get a huge overload just sitting behind a screen. Also, during those teenage years, changes in both dopamine and serotonin make adolescents more emotional and more responsive to reward. The increase in dopamine activity in adolescence may also have implications for risk-taking and their vulnerability to boredom. By adolescence, we should have already learned the skills we need for survival, and nature herself would satiate the risk, reward and our vulnerability to boredom. I noticed this with our girls: when Lola hit 11, I was hearing comments like, 'I don't know what to do with myself at the moment, I'm bored.' Suddenly, she's got to go and seek that dopamine hit. But the seeking of dopamine can be found through play. We just have to 're-child' by hiding (the screen) and seeking (the dopamine).

But what we are missing in these isolated spikes of biological stimulation is the cocktail effect that lets us shake up to wake up all of these individual neurochemicals and many more, in unison. Can you imagine being able to tap into the euphoria of the runners' high combined with a giant enveloping hug whenever you choose? Or being able to deconstruct stagnant trauma though accessing your primal pathways? And – you guessed it – play is the hand that gives these hormone ingredients a good shaking.

I want you to use your playful imagination now, just for a moment. Join me in flow state.

Think deep and dig up those repressed urges to explore your body, mind and environment as the ultimate playgrounds.

Given that socially normal walking is actually kind of boring, I want you to picture the endless ways in which you could use your body to get from one place to another.

Where would you travel to in your mind, what feelings would you rouse if you kicked down your social conditioning and expanded your restricted approach to your environment?

Explore how it would feel to spontaneously bust out some act of physical silliness, just because you had an internal urge to honour your mental and physical freedom.

Steps to rewilding your moving and playing

So let's start the rewilding and re-childing process and transform those shoe-shaped feet to the phenomenal foundations of your superstructure.

REBOOT YOUR POSTURE
Fundamental to rebooting your posture is creating a solid ground-sitting practice. The postures in which we choose to rest on the floor help feed and nourish complex and extraordinary wild shapes. Although there are a large number of different rest positions to choose from, I have narrowed my approach down to just six wild, posture-enhancing shapes, each containing several variations, here.

They should help towards liberating your ankles, knees, hips, spine, shoulders and neck from the chair and get your all-important power poses fired up!

Each one of these resting positions offers its own unique code for postural wellbeing and growth and you soon get the signal from your body to change position and eliminate stagnation (a biological cue we disconnect from when we sit in chairs). This means you're continually uploading sensory gains while you work, rest or play.

The six rest positions

An easy movement gain is to choose any of these ground-resting positions and work from the ground to rebuild your body's connection to its natural state.

Try to incorporate these moves into your day, every day: perhaps practise a few of them first thing each morning, or make some time to reconnect to your body every evening. If you work from home, intersperse your working day with a movement break each hour to ground you, physically and mentally.

The same goes for correcting your typing and swiping patterns. When you're bingeing on Netflix, try watching a box set shifting between some of these positions rather than lounging on the sofa.

It may feel very uncomfortable and awkward at first: this is just because your body isn't used to it. Persevere and remember to breathe, and very soon you will begin to find ease and comfort.

This way, you avoid the unhealthy sitting position and upload your floor-sitting practice, making you much more likely to remember to keep up the new habits daily – which is what you need for long 'standing' change. If the kids want to watch CBeebies or hit the iPad, make the terms of the screen time a mash-up of shape-shifting, too.

POSITION 1: KNEELING

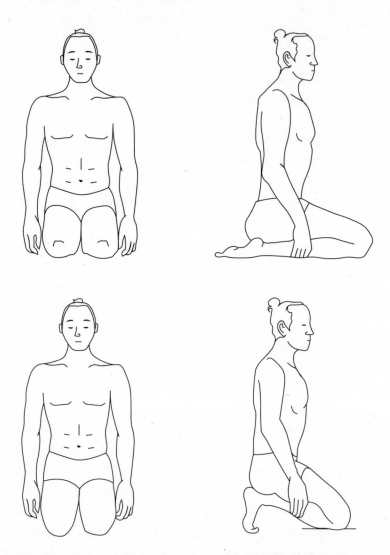

POSITION 2: SINGLE LEG KNEELING

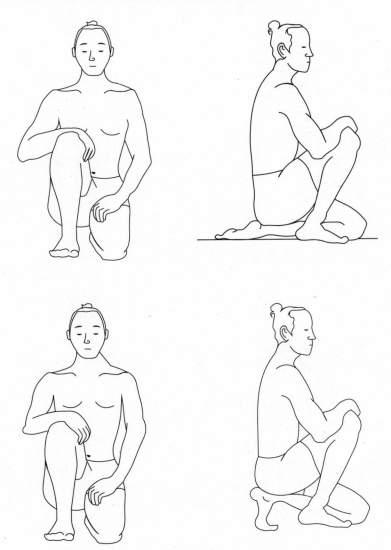

POSITION 3: SIDE-SITTING SERIES

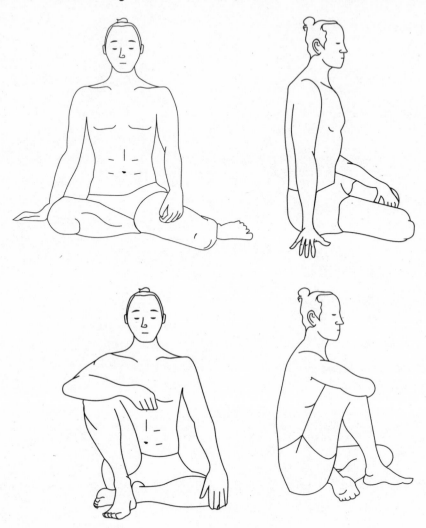

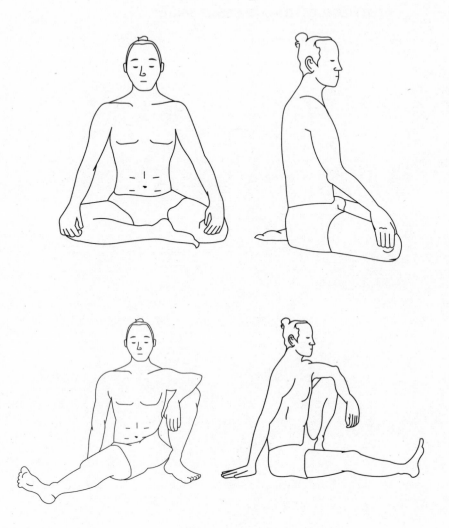

POSITION 4: LONG-SITTING SERIES

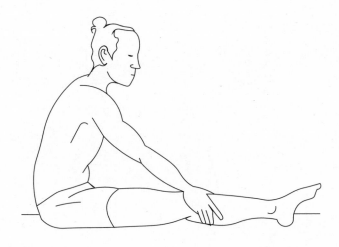

POSITION 5: TUCK AND HOLD SITTING

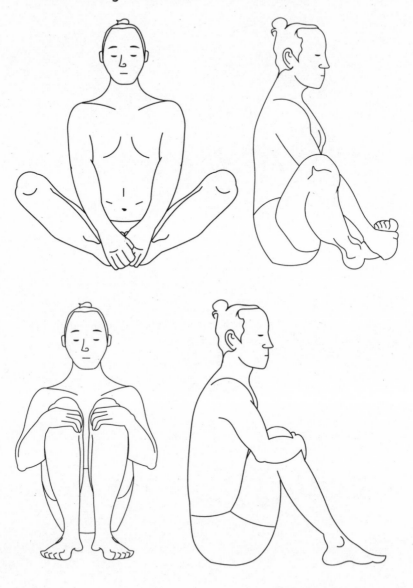

POSITION 6: SQUATTING

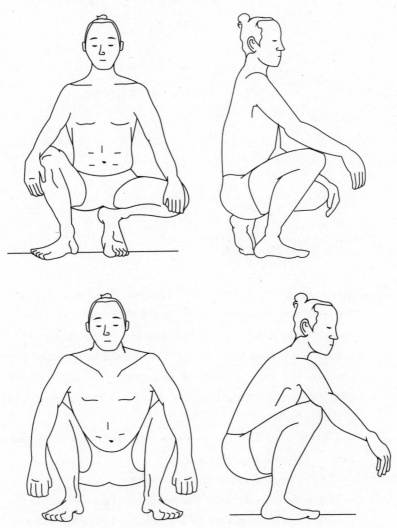

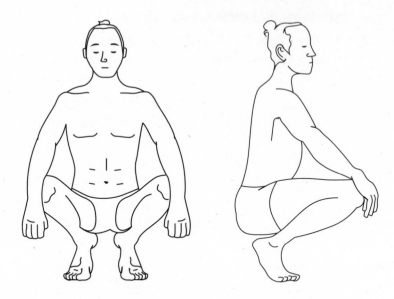

Squatting is a rest position in nature that allows us to maintain the same body weight through the soles of our feet to the earth, compared to when we stand on two feet. I see the squat as a fundamental foundation to my own barefoot endurance athleticism, but I do not view it as exercise. It's a playful rest position of subconscious choice that I will now choose over sitting in a chair.

- During your Netflix marathon, avoid the chair and upload your ground-resting practices.
- Choose to read your emails in a squat.
- If you don't quite have the ankle function to reach a flat-footed squat, drop a wedge behind your heel and, over time, reduce the height of the wedge.

BECOME AN OPPORTUNIST MOVER

Being an opportunist mover helps you get grounded, gain some sensory feedback and upgrade your movement potential by incorporating it into the activities you're already doing.

- To rewild your feet, get into a habit of using your otherwise static toothbrushing time to do your Toega (page 82).

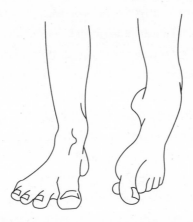

- Instead of walking around that patch of green grass you usually pass on your way to work, free your feet out of their shoe cages and walk on the grass to connect to the earth.

REWILD YOUR FOOTWEAR

With just a simple switch, you'll reap the benefits of neurological and sensory uploads, just from wearing appropriately foot-shaped footwear. If you're already an avid member of the 10,000-steps-a-day club, this switch will transform your body, too. By rewilding your footwear, you rewild your walk, which in turn helps fire up those wild walking muscular systems and your wild posture.

- Check out Vivobarefoot and you won't look back.

SQUAT, HANG AND SURF IN PUBLIC

You can change your perceptions of your surroundings and begin to think like a rewilder: 'Ah, there's a bar above my head, I'm going to grab that and hang with my weight!', 'Let's see if I can rest in squat each time the train stops and hang as we travel from station to station!' Choosing to raise some socially extreme eyebrows might make you feel vulnerable at first, but thwarting social rules that inhibit our natural gains is the best way to elicit the change towards natural norms – and you may alter some perceptions and inspire a few people along the way!

- Instead of holding on to a rail for support, or sitting, stand on the Tube or train. Ground through your feet, stacking your head, chest and pelvis above your base of support (your feet) and surf, using your biomechanics for stability.
- Once you're done with your train surfing and Tube-stop squat, raise the intensity game with escalator runs, or by taking the stairs instead of the lift.

STAND AT YOUR DESK

Another great upload into our habitat – and gaining some socially normal credits – is the standing desk. If your HR department will allow it, this can be a game changer. I say can be, because standing in one spot for hours can be just as detrimental as sitting if you have poor posture and compromising footwear. So the key is to remember to break up any stationary position with movement, as much as you can.

- In conjunction with standing desks, I recommend tuning into your feet and posture by regularly practising the posture squat.

- Keep rebooting the relationship between your phenomenal feet, ankles, knees, hips and pelvis – the foundations from which to build your straight spine and superstructure.

OFFSET YOUR CHAIR SITTING

Where the office chair becomes an unavoidable sitting scenario, I recommend the posture squat technique. This is about creating an upright posture, so keep your chest up and your eyes level on the horizon and don't worry too much about keeping your heels down. In fact, give your ankles a break by allowing your heels to rise up.

- Do five posture squats and you're now movement-ready and can walk off like a human!
- Why don't you use a timer while at your desk to remind you to intermittently move and change shape; remember you are a human animal with movement needs. When the timer sounds, slide your chair back, place your hands on top of the desk for an anterior support and squat down. Focus in on your big toes as grounding anchors.

WORK FROM THE GROUND

An easy movement gain for the working day is to work from the ground with your laptop, mashing your movement with your work.

- Choose any of the ground-resting positions. Each offers its own unique code for postural wellbeing and growth.
- Change position. You soon get the signal from your body to change position, meaning you're continually uploading positive sensory gains while you work.

MAKE TIME FOR HANGING

Gripping and hanging are part of our natural human movement repertoire of climbing and arm swinging, helping to organize our posture, allowing our ribcage to lift and expand to improve our respiratory system and nerve function.

- Fitting a low-cost (or high-cost) pull-up bar in one of your door frames is a great tool to help unravel the upper body from all the swiping and typing-induced postural dysfunction.
- Set your smartphone timer and work towards hanging for 30–60 seconds at a time, at intervals, to break up your working day. Perhaps drop into a squat in the rest between hangs.

GET OUT WELL

If you drive a lot, or have to drive to meetings or commute by car, I recommend the same posture squat method for when you get out of the car. For my clients who fly frequently I advise setting a timer to encourage them to keep moving throughout the flight.

- Car: step out of the car and use the door frame as support to upload your posture squat before you walk off.
- Aircraft: to save yourself all manner of back trouble, the most important thing to get right is what you do when leaving the plane. As soon as you get out of your seat, before reaching for your suitcase, do a little reboot with your posture squat in the aisle. This is super-important for your hips and spine before you load yourself up with your carry-on.

SHAKE TO UNBREAK (OR SHAKEN, NOT STIRRED)

Shaking is a primal impulse, offering a naturally playful way to release trauma and is one of the simplest ways to release stress.

- Stand with your head, chest and pelvis aligned. Relax your jaw, shoulders and belly. Tune into the pads of your feet, soften your knees. Starting from the floor, drive a pulse up through your body. I want you to feel as if the heels of your feet are ever so slightly tapping the ground. From your feet, to your ankles, to your knees, drive this same pulse. Now inhale for four pulses and exhale for four pulses and maintain this tempo of breath throughout your pulsing play.

- Allow your shoulders to bob up and down and your elbows and hands to move around freely with the same heel pulse. Think of your joints and tissues softening. Feel into your muscles being able to shake free of the bones. Now allow this feeling of pulsing to intensify, working your way up from the floor to your cheeks and jaw; let those healing vibrations shake off your tension.

RE-CHILD

In transforming your movement gains into playful movement gains, you are literally changing your creative mind as well as your body, stirring up those all-important hormones associated with happiness. Give yourself permission to move and play out under the big blue sky – climbing trees, balancing on curbstones or rails, jumping, leaping, rolling, crawling or running barefoot over the frosty grass. Surprise yourself with as much physical, spiritual and emotional expression as wildly possible.

- Got kids? Really raise the wild vibes by playing animal movement tag – whoever's 'It' chooses the animal. If it's a cat, then off you all go playing tag on all fours as cats.
- Another favourite to help shake out the working-from-home funk is to set a timer for each hour of work and then whack on a banging tune to lose your sh*t to.

NEXT » EATING AND DRINKING

- Learn how it's going to take guts to rewild your eating habits.
- Understand the importance of down-regulating through what you absorb.
- Take back control of your palate.

CHAPTER 6

Eating and Drinking

In this chapter we're going to be looking deeply into eating and drinking in rewilding terms. But, perhaps surprisingly, this isn't going to be a prescriptive chapter about what you should eat and how to overhaul your diet. Instead, I'll be asking you to look after your gut and think about what you're absorbing. I will explore various different types of diet and the ethos around nourishment; this chapter invites curiosity about how diet, and the integrity of our food, affects our physiology and mental strength. I will share what works for me, with a view to you then exploring what works for *you*. You'll be considering toxins vs nourishment, understanding the benefits of down-regulating and mindfully tuning into your personal human needs. Take account of your habitat and environment, as indigenous cultures have done, and you'll soon be trying to reconnect to a better kind of relationship with your food.

To live is to encounter stress. When stressed, some people eat more, others eat less. The trouble is, when this response is in place, our digestion isn't functioning for either eventuality. Thus, the necessary absorption cannot take place. This begins to make more sense when we apply our domesticated, urbanite, zoo lens to this – hitting all the red lights on the school drop, navigating the commute when late for work, having that stressful meeting with the boss. (Fill in the box with your own stressor here.) So, really, this chapter isn't about eating and drinking at all, it's about what affects our absorption.

You are not what you eat – you are what you absorb.

Before moving forward with this chapter, I'm going to ask you to sit and breathe. When it comes to food, we can often be triggered, especially if we feel it's threatening our beliefs, or our inherited templates of foods. We have a lot of emotional attachment to food and this chapter may challenge some of these deeply held addictions. When that happens, the walls can go up – suddenly we're no longer hearing, seeing or feeling; or in this case, reading. This is an opportunity to go back and see food and drink from a beginner's mindset, through an authentic lens – an empty cup and an empty bowl. Let's try it. We're going to use one of the down-regulating breath practices from the Breathing and Being chapter: 5 seconds in, 8 seconds out.

Drawing the breath in through the nose, then letting out a long exhale, we just sit and breathe. It can be three minutes, or four can be fine – whatever you feel it needs in that moment for you to feel down-regulated before entering the chapter. When you reach a point in this chapter where you feel your beliefs being challenged, or you have an emotional reaction to the content, just sit back and breathe for a moment, before moving on. Again, allow yourself to see it through those authentic eyes.

Being human takes guts

Mounting evidence suggests that the richer and more diverse the community of microbes in your gut, the lower your risk of myriad modern-day diseases, including mental ill health. The biodiversity of our soils not only holds the key to rewilding our lifestyles and what we eat but is essential to the thriving biodiversity of our microbiome, or our 'gut garden'. Like the microbial soil, your microbiome is this huge community that is constantly in communication, and it way outnumbers our trillions of human cells. Scientific opinions vary – some say we are 10% human, but most align in saying that *more than half your body is not human*, but is made up of microbes and other microorganisms. Hold that thought for a second or two.

This vast microbiome community plays a huge role in influencing your metabolism, immune system and mood. Yes, your mood! You are not just what you eat. You are also what your microbiome eats. And your mood is impacted by the diversity of your microbiome. Imagine that on a multi-personality level – trillions of bacteria having constant meetings on how your mood should play out.

So, before we even talk about what you eat and drink, let's get down and dirty in the soil and understand the evolution of the human diet and the way we digest our food. I'm going to begin by exposing the evolution of the human diet and the foundation of my food philosophy learned through time spent with my Wild Fitness family.

EVOLUTION OF HUMAN DIGESTION

30 million years as Primates:

- Soils rich in fungal and microbial biodiversity
- Ratio: 95% herbivorous/frugivorous, 5% wild animal protein from small mammals, eggs and opportunistic insect and termite uptake
- Majority of dietary needs provided by fermentation of plant-based foods by enzymes and bacterial metabolism
- Fibre intake is approximately 300g per day

6 million years as Hominins (divergence of quadrupedal plant-based ape to bipedal scavenger primate):

- Soils rich in fungal and microbial diversity
- Ratio: 80% plant-based, 20% higher wild animal protein uptake from small mammals, insects and scavenging carcasses for tendons, ligaments, marrow, meat scrap
- Colonic fermentation contributing up to 50% of dietary needs
- Fibre intake of 200g per day

200,000–400,000 years as sophisticated hunter-gatherers:

- Soils rich in fungal and microbial biodiversity
- Ratio: 65–70% plant based, 30–35% wild animal protein, depending on geographic location and hunting success
- Minimum of 30% calories coming from protein from wild animals
- Minimum of 30% calories coming from fats from wild animals
- Fibre intake of 100g per day from a predominately plant-based diet

10,000 years as farmers:

- First declining shift in soil and food biodiversity
- Introduction of grain, whole grain, pseudo grain, modified plants
- Introduction of dairy and farmed livestock meat
- High phytate content, inhibiting absorption
- Fibre intake of 30–50g per day from grain crops, foraged and grown plants

100 years consuming a zoo diet:

- Exhausted soils used for monocropping and sprayed with pesticides
- Livestock animals pumped with antibiotics and synthetic hormones and fed on pesticide-sprayed monocrops
- Genetically modified food crops, exterminating insects and bees essential for biodiversity
- Proliferation of processed 'fake' convenience foods with added salts, sugars, fats, supplements
- Gut dysbioisis from antibiotics in food chain and lack of prebiotic and symbiotic foods
- Fibre intake 10–20g per day

It doesn't require a lot of imagination to see that, consuming the zoo diet, our food template is slightly off here. That, given the current state of the relationship between soils and foods, anyone could struggle to get their most basic of needs met, easily falling into the trap of becoming overfed but undernourished.

Food forgetfulness

Peter H. Kahn, a professor in the University of Washington's Department of Psychology, and Director of the Human Interaction With Nature and Technological Systems (HINTS) Lab, presented an idea called 'environmental generational amnesia': each generation is born into a new social norm and will perceive the environment into which it's born, no matter how unnatural, as *their normal*. So what each generation comes to think of as the 'norm' is simply based on what they're experiencing it to be.

Let's apply Peter Kahn's environmental generational amnesia to our food. When I was born 45 years ago, we had 60% more wildlife than we do today. My son Bow's experience of wildlife is 60% less than mine. If we apply the same 60% wildlife decline to our soils and foods – and absorption of those soils and foods – we're now aware of the impact this will have on our gut health through the generations.

The presence of alcohol, sugars and other mind- and mood-altering zoo foods also has negative effects on our ability to tune in to *what we actually need*. Not just in our intuitive food decision-making process, but in our everyday lifestyle choices, contributing to physical, mental, emotional and spiritual disconnection. Just think of the origins of the sugar industry and how the trade of this white gold enslaved and disempowered so many.

Our chronic stress and our approach to food has also changed in that time without our noticing it. More specifically, consider the soils in which our foods are grown. It's here that I think one of Khan's quotes really hits the spot.

'With each ensuing generation, the amount of environmental degradation increases, but each generation tends to perceive that degraded condition as the non-degraded condition, as the normal experience.'

Peter H. Kahn

Looking at the soils in which my two-year-old son's veggies are grown today – compared to the soils in which my foods were grown at his age – we can understand the potential impact on our growth of decades of nutrient depletion. Soils are too often mono-cropped, grown in the same field, drawing up the same nutrients over and over again. This new norm of soil degradation is at odds with our nutritional needs at the basic nourishment level. *Peter Kahn's model is not only fantastic for highlighting the importance of regenerative farming and the rewilding of our lands for generations to come*, it also enables us, individually, to take control where we *can* take control. As well as work on our own rebalancing and down-regulation, we badly need to regenerate and rewild our digestive system. Down-regulating your nervous system can be a huge game changer for digestion, which in turn is influenced by your emotional choices and responses to food and eating, but also for tuning into your food needs and managing your pacifying Western wants.

WHY DOWN-REGULATION IS IMPORTANT

With digestion, down-regulation is key. Not only does it enable the 'digest', it also helps to reboot our sympathetic/parasympathetic nervous system response. The sympathetic division initiates the fight-or-flight response and the parasympathetic division initiates the rest-and-digest responses in the brain.

- Mother Nature has excelled herself in creating our gut lining. This extraordinary gatekeeper to our cellular kingdom allows only the good in and keeps out the bad particles and toxins. It's a dance with equilibrium that relies heavily on how we're connected to the vast microbial and fungal networks of our Mother Earth.

- Think back to those tribes at one within the environment, who do not see themselves as separate from nature, moving through a landscape. Everything they engage with on a sensory level – breathing, touching, seeing, eating – all keeps this symbiotic dance going, reaffirming that we are not just what we eat, we are ultimately what we absorb.

- You, your habits and your habitat are intertwined with your health and emotional wellbeing. If you live in the Human Zoo and are divorced from nature, without practising any down-regulating practices, this will affect your ability to produce the right stomach acids and enzymes.

- Think of this in the context of an up-regulated versus down-regulated absorption and what we now know happens when we're out of balance and the impact on our regulatory systems.

- Down-regulation practices – breath, meditation, even bowing your head in gratitude for what's on your plate – prepare the digestive system for food. Not blocking your sensory reception of food with screens, so you can *see* your food, means that your digestive enzymes fully understand what is about to be received. This also helps you honour your natural food needs over your emotional food wants.

- There's another important factor that resides inside and outside our human self – our microbiome. This is our gut microbiome, 'gut garden' or, as I now see it, our 'foragers' forest.'

This microbial organ influences your metabolism, immune system, digestion and mood: in order to align with our authentic nature we will need to rewild the gut.

- And, of course, the more nature we nourish our microbial community with, the more natural the outcome this can play in distributing the wealth of nutrients we so greatly need to thrive.

Abraham Maslow published *Hierarchy of Needs* in 1943, a pyramid diagram in which he established that in order to survive and thrive, human beings have to fulfil certain needs within categories, beginning with the most fundamental for survival (at the bottom), to the needs that promote growth and thriving (at the top): physiological needs, safety, belongingness and love, esteem and self-actualization (fulfilment of potential).

I apply nature as a filter to this hierarchy, looking to modern hunter-gatherer tribes that have been minimally exposed to modern living as an example. Without doubt, they have the same physical, social and spiritual needs as we urbanites, despite our chair-using, technology-driven, monocropped, processed food-eating lives of convenience.

Can we truly satisfy our base-level physiological need for nourishment, if our food system is of substandard quality, grown in depleted soil, fed on antibiotics, sprayed with pesticides, created in a factory, wrapped up in toxic packaging, shipped thousands of miles to reach us, has a shelf life years long, and is then heated up in a microwave? Is this 'Maslow food need' truly being met? Are we not forever falling short of meeting this need for nourishment? How can we strive for the zenith of self-actualization, when we're all the time distracted, scratching away in the degraded, depleted soils at the bottom of the pyramid?

If your fundamental need for natural food isn't being met, you'll be filling in that void with another distraction, as a response to absorbing a huge toxic load. It's a vicious cycle. The more disconnected your food is from nature, the less likely your nourishment need will be met. On an intellectual level, you'll be able to tell yourself that you enjoyed the food and it filled your belly. But on the level of your *cellular, microbial and energy systems*, you're adding to your human suffering.

So, if your reaction to pacifying your stress is to feed, you will keep feeding. If you keep feeding on the same food group from the same zoo/laboratory plate, then you're perpetuating the cycle. Once you become aware of this, you might begin to understand that you're *out of balance*, not regulated. Use this as a point to check in and think for a moment. Why is it that I'm not in balance?

Once you are closer to satisfying your human needs on this cellular level, however, you can genuinely live in biologically normal happiness and begin to move up the pyramid towards thriving.

Food takeaway: if you want to tune into being this innately wild, connected and empowered being nature intended you to be, then you have to eat like an innately, wild, connected and empowered being. Food for manifesting thought, don't you think?

With nourishment, we have choices

If I choose Human Zoo food (overprocessed, air-freighted, mass-produced), then I know on many levels that it's toxic. Is it growth-promoting or is it compromising? If it's not good for me, or it's not good for the environment, then it's certainly not good for the next generation to observe and inherit.

What would be better: a highly nutritious diet but a compromised digestion, or a terrible diet but a better digestion system? This was the question my good friend and wellness guru, Jasmine Hemsley, posed to me. She went on to explain that it is, of course, much more important that you get your digestion in check first, then clean your diet up. Work on down-regulating, rest-and-DIGEST practices that help prime the digestive system for absorption.

As well as my Wild Fitness community and Jasmine, a handful of other people have helped flip my eating and drinking switch. I met world-renowned Raw Vegan Chef Diego Castro on a plant medicine retreat. He introduced me and my tribe to eating more raw and fermented foods and to the term 'flexitarian', which is an increasingly popular way of approaching a plant-based diet that's mostly plants, yet allows for the occasional consciously chosen meat dish. Better for health = better for the planet. Diego taught us to simply be more *flexi* overall, opting more often than not for natural, wild and organic foods. I draw on Diego's inspiration of this 'flexi' approach when traversing between the primate, hominin and hunter-gatherer stages of our evolution.

Intuitive vs habit

When living in Ibiza, I met the Viking. He's huge, with a big beard and long hair and has sailed solo from Ibiza to Australia. The Viking's diet is predominately plant-based, but when travelling in cities, he says he *feels the need* to eat more meat. He often practises extreme periods of fasting – fasting is a contentious subject and I would advise you to do your research before you embark on any fasting pro-gramme, to find out what works for you. It struck me after conversing with him that our attitude towards nutrition is governed as much by habit, habitats and our emotional response as it is by real hunger. We inherit so much from our tribes of influence and literally navigate through much of our life eating the same food at the same time, with the same templates for breakfast, lunch and dinner and using food as a pacifier to deal with the stresses of our environment.

Fasting like the Viking out in nature, away from my device and the 'doing' vibes of the city, allowed me the space and time to real-ize that my 'need to feed hunger' was a symptom of stressful doing, and that zoo foods were my pacifying want, masking a hunger for something other than food, for what my true emotions might be. I now take inspiration from the Viking; if I'm craving zoo foods or booze, it's highlighting that something is out of balance. I will fast fortnightly for 24 hours and use breath and nature immersion to help me tune into my needs. If I'm feeling a little stuck or 'imposter addict Tony' drops in for an internal chatter, then I'll throw in another 24-hour fast for a complete reboot.

More plants, less meat

One of my big-time inspirations is plant-based ultra-athlete Rich Roll, who helped me see beyond my 'animal proteins for training gains' mindset and encouraged me to add more plants to my plate. More importantly, he got me to quit the pacifying booze and drugs out of my diet by recognizing that my abuse was neither serving me nor allowing me to reach my fulfilled potential. Rich helped me to hold the all-important space of being an authentic, connected human, husband and parent, as well as performing in the world of endurance running.

Optimize your omegas

Dr Terry Wahls is a clinical professor of medicine and author of *The Wahls Protocol* and is renowned worldwide for defeating her own progressive multiple sclerosis through nutrition. She was presenting slides of images of herself in a wheelchair when her illness was at its most crippling, discussing how she'd studied cellular biology to learn what to feed her cells and mitochondria (the powerhouses of our cells, the root of our energy) to heal herself to a disease-free state. She did so by improving her 'omega 3 to 6 ratio' by completely removing high omega 6 processed zoo foods and processed grains and grain-fed animals from her diet. Mass-farmed animals are fed grain, creating an inflamed, suffering animal; they are often also fed antibiotics, which all drips into our physiology and inflammation. Dr Wahls introduced an abundance of phytonutrients (plants) to her plate. We're not talking just five a day here. We're talking three cups of veggies per day and lots of sulphur- and iodine-rich foods, such as seaweed, wakame, onions, garlic, mushrooms. Dr Wahls shows how crucial it is to consider our cellular nourishment when looking at our overall health, preventative medicine and vitality. Before hitting 40 I hadn't considered the importance of nourishing my mitochondria for powering me through the day.

While the Wild Fitness evolution of the human diet template pointed me in the right direction, all these people helped flip a perception-shifting switch in me that enabled me to relearn how to eat and perform like a cellular, microbial, energetic, connected Tony.

Learning from indigenous people's relationship to our Earth

As mentioned earlier, indigenous people comprise less than 5% of the world population yet they protect 80% of global biodiversity. Both numbers are declining. The industrialization of humanity has seen global wildlife populations drop by 60% since 1970, just over half a century ago. This is more than half the lifespan of us modern-day urbanites. More tragically, our natural humanity is disappearing at an alarming rate. If we wipe out the protectors of our ecosystem, what will our global biodiversity look like in another half century? Worse still, if we wipe out the natural beings of this world, we lose the most important templates of all – *what it is to live naturally and to co-exist in our natural world.* We lose the profound wisdom of how indigenous people protect such a sophisticated ecosystem. And we lose our natural templates for the most fundamental needs of all: eating and drinking. We need to do better.

THE HADZA

Let's visit the Hadza, a tribe in Tanzania. They are one of the last remaining hunter-gatherer-forager groups in Africa, living out their days in the same way as our pre-agricultural sapiens ancestors did for thousands of years.

The Hadza people's microbiome is considered to be one of the most diverse on the planet. Interestingly, there is a difference between the microbiome of Hadza women and Hadza men. Women keep the camp in check, keeping the community vibes high; they forage for fibre-rich tubers and plant foods. Men, on the other hand, interact with the elements far away from camp.

They forage to catch game meat, honey and plants including tubers, berries and baobab. There are parts of the animals eaten solely by the men and certain meats eaten solely by the women and children.

This means that male and female Hadza groups are growing and maintaining different gut gardens. They represent the pinnacle of authentic natural lifestyles – moving, sleeping, playing, eating naturally and mindfully from the plant and animal kingdoms and interacting with their diverse soils. The Hadza have very little to no medicine. They consume no farmed monocrop from depleted soils or any of our processed food products.

We cannot underestimate the profound influence that the foundation of our gut and its vast microbial network has on our human health and wellbeing. In the same breath, we must recognize just how our behaviours, lifestyles and environments influence the foundation of our gut and our microbial network.

Foraging for your food is an incredibly mindful practice. It stimulates us physically and spiritually, encouraging us to stay present in the moment. Foraging will give you the most incredible neurological, physiological and emotional gains. The more exposure to the experience, the more gains. 'Foraging' may feel far removed from the urban existence, but there are ways we can bring in elements of foraging even to the highest of city apartment blocks. Creating your own regenerative veggie or herb plot on a window box will drop you into a rest-and-digest state, and this will feed you as a whole, not just your belly. Getting your hands and bare feet down in the dirt – actually let's call it soil, not dirt – will stimulate an emotional and microbial conversation between the soil, your foods and your belly, where your senses come alive and your digestive system primes for absorption. And it is this exact harmonious relationship between the absorbent sensory human and the soil that excites and inspires me the most.

Our Paleolithic ancestors didn't experience the chronic environmental and lifestyle-inducing stresses that we are experiencing today. But they were, of course, living in pretty hostile times, too. Theirs would have been different types of stress – acute and immediate, not chronic and persistent.

Neither our Primate ancestors, nor our scavenging Hominid cousins, nor our hunter-gatherer forebears were experiencing anything near what we zoo humans have had to endure: processed zoo foods; sensory deprivation; nature deficit disorders; inappropriate, undernourishing, compromising movement; electromagnetic waves; toxic light pollution and lack of natural light wreaking havoc on our circadian rhythm; air and noise pollution; traffic and commuter chaos; social disconnection . . . I could continue, but I feel you getting up-regulated. Let me just say that, compared to our ancestors, *we have a completely flipped and distorted parasympathetic–sympathetic ratio.*

While we can't exactly determine what that ancient landscape was like, hostile or not, we can look to the indigenous peoples of today, especially those that are still living their most authentically human ways. We can also look to our closest DNA cousins – the chimpanzee and bonobo – to see what things might have looked like in our most herbivorous, frugivorous, pre-divergence, predominantly plant-based days. We can also turn to agricultural tribes to see what farming might have looked like when we were bridging the gap between *being* the ecosystem and *living* independent of it.

We can see that they play out their days in a down-regulated, para-sympathetic, rest-and-digest, meditative state. They only enter the stressed-out state when there's imminent danger – but still, it's an acute, not a chronic response.

Here's the evolutionary kicker. It doesn't matter how far down the phylogenic tree we climb, the *stress response remains the same*. It is designed to deal with the *immediate* threat. I call this 'the lion in the room'. If the lion is in the room with you, your survival brain will trigger an *acute* response: fight or flight. So what happens when said lion comes a-strolling into the room?

1) Fight?
2) Flight?

Choose number 2 and it really does mean a number 2. I would mess my paleo pants: my digestive system would pause. The communication between the brain and digestive tract (gut–brain axis) is interrupted, from digestive muscles to stomach acid and digestive enzymes. There's no point in digesting anything right now; it uses up energy when we just need to run. My gonads would shrivel up. No need for them, reproduction is definitely out of the equation when it's not safe. My immune system will shut down . . . no point in fighting off Covid while the lion's breathing down my neck. So can you imagine what would happen if the lion, instead of being an *acute* stressor, the modern-day lion – your mortgage demands, an irritable commute, a demanding boss – becomes a *chronic stressor*? The important thing is that your three main regulatory systems – digestive, hormonal and immune – will pause while you run from that lion. But in modern life, we never actually get away, so there is no release for the nervous system.

Does this sound familiar? Think of the myriad health conditions that we urbanites experience today and you can slot them into the digestive, hormonal and immune regulatory boxes. If we remain in protection mode, our bodies are simply not functioning well enough. We actually create the perfect environment for digestive issues, anxiety, disease, malaise – all the disaffections that plague modern life.

You are your habitat

Whether we live in the Human Laboratory or in the forests, in a wild tribe or in a 21st-century city, our bodies, minds, health and happiness are ultimately determined by our surroundings. I interviewed Isabella Tree, author of *Wilding* and partner to Sir Charles Burrell of the Knepp Castle estate in the UK. For the last 20 years, they have been regenerating the estate and rewilding their land. Today, rare species like nightingales, falcons, owls, turtle doves, beavers and bats are thriving and grazing animals are left to roam freely, with no veterinary intervention.

Isabella explained that if they were to cut back or prune a plant, it would grow back thicker – indeed, it's one of the productive techniques used in horticulture. However, when an animal grazes on shrubs, shoots or small branches, something different happens in nature. It's as if there's communication between the animals' saliva and the shoots, plants and bushes. Shrubs grow back thicker and at a much faster rate, to provide the animals with what they need.

This connected me to another conversation, with the queen of regenerative farming and soil biodiversity, Abby Rose. We'd talked about the communication between plants and soil; how, through photosynthesis, the plant lays down sugars through its roots into the soil and, in return, the soil gives the plant the nutrients it needs. Mind-blowing, right!?

Both conversations with Isabella and Abby left me curious as to what communication has been lost when we stopped getting our hands and bare feet down in the soil.

Climbing down the phylogenic tree

Now, let's return to the 5% of the world population – or, more specifically, the indigenous tribes who are moving and foraging in their flow states. Just for a moment, imagine what their communication with their environment must be like and what it must have been like when *all* humans were hunter-gatherers, hunter-horticulturists, foragers, foresters and defenders of the world's biodiversity.

Think how mindful these beings are: they are the environment, not separate from it; they are the plants, the rocks, the animals. They are the vibration of it all, beautiful beings of planet breath. They move like down-regulated, rested-and-digested beings, primed for absorbing all of nature's nutrients, the ultimate symbiotic relationship. We zoo humans, on the other hand, traverse our linear landscape in a sensory-deprived, up-regulated, stressed and possessed, absorption-inhibiting way.

This can be a little difficult for our disconnected and domesticated human minds to comprehend. So let's go back to before the birth of growing monocrop grain, when we were part of that same biodiversity that is today being protected by just 5% of us. Can you begin to feel that we too were once these amazing beings, hooked up to the fungal and microbial networks, walking barefoot, our hands and skin in deep connection with the soil, the bush, the shrubs and fruits?

Bring that recognition back to the present. It paints a very different picture to diving into the supermarket and grabbing some processed zoo foods to feed the latest dietary fad, then mindlessly wolfing them down while scrolling the 'gram in an unregulated stressed state, all in hope of feeling full, but very unlikely feeling fulfilled.

It is, in fact, our environment and what we consume from it which controls our health and wellbeing, right down to cellular behaviour. To better understand what this means, let's visit the work of Bruce Lipton on epigenetics, the study of how our behaviour and environment can cause changes to the way our genes work.

Lipton's explorations into cell biology and cellular behaviour were pivotal in my awakening and largely informed my teachings on my first retreat programmes. His work enabled me to make that important connection between the human needs which Maslow put forth and how they fall short of satisfying us as biological beings in the modern world.

As a cellular biologist, Lipton discovered that the outer layer of every single one of the nearly 40 trillion cells in our bodies has its own intelligence, *meaning it can learn*. Not only can our cells learn, they can be consciously and subconsciously *controlled by us*. In a revolutionary experiment, Lipton took three identical groups of stem cells from the same Petri dish, cultured each group into its own Petri dish and allowed the cells to grow within chemically different environments. The introduction of these different culture mediums to the Petri dishes saw the cells in one dish form muscle, another form bone and the third form fat cells. What makes this experiment so profound is that it proved, through the three different fates of the originally identical groups of cells, that our genetics are actually not predetermined. We might have certain predispositions, but it is our inherited habits and habitats that allow them to become pre-determined. We are taught that genes control life, that the genes we arrive in this world with control our bodily fates, yet here was Bruce Lipton definitively proving otherwise.

Contrary to mainstream belief, our biology is not genetically predetermined. What you put into your own Petri dish, your environment, is responsible for how you either thrive or survive as an organism. Your fate rests not on your genetics, but on whether your dish is filled with toxins or nourishment. When I found this study, it's no exaggeration to say that it tantalized my then sick, negatively charged, pseudo-realized mind enough to change my career direction from that point on. More than that – my physical, emotional and spiritual self was irrevocably transformed, too.

If we know that our cells are compromised by toxins, and they're going to protection state, that's our *whole human system in that protection state*. If the microbiome is in dysbiosis, then our whole human and microbial system is compromised and our mood is adversely affected, too.

More profound still was Lipton's discovery that the protection and growth states of cells could also be controlled even after their environments had induced sickness. Lipton also found that taking a Petri dish of healthy cells and moving it from a healthy to a toxic environment caused the cells to enter a state of protection and become sick. Refusing to heal the sick cells with drugs, as is standard practice for biologists, he then discovered something even more profound. Simply removing the dish from the unhealthy, toxic environment and returning it back to a healthy environment was enough for the cells to naturally regain growth by themselves.

What this means for us is that, if we introduce a toxic property to our personal Petri dish – in this case food – we create an environment which instigates protection. When we're exposed to environmental toxins – as we are with most of the zoo foods we consume today – we remain in protection mode.

What we choose to nourish ourselves with drives the growth state of self-actualization. The growth state is the right environment to meet all of our fundamental needs. We cannot be simultaneously in protection and growth mode. Lipton's work helped me understand why we have to remove the toxicity from our living environments, from the soil we grow our foods in, to the foods we choose to culture in our human Petri dish. We are responsible for this, collectively and individually.

Made up of trillions and trillions of cells, every one of us is essentially a walking version of Lipton's Petri dishes. But we alone are the ones responsible for the messages they are exposed to by our surroundings and our own thoughts and beliefs. We are the scientific controllers of our own huge, fleshy, bipedal Petri dishes. By nature, it would be biologically normal for us to swing between the two states of protection and growth. We see this all the time in wild animals, as they alternate between states of fight or flight, freeze and rest, digest and play within their natural habitats, enabling them to grow.

It should be the same for us. In times of fear, we know that the digestive, immune and hormonal systems go into protection mode – blood is sent from our digestive organs out to extremities, enabling us to run or fight for our lives. Once it is safe, the biologically normal animal will quickly process and move on from its traumatic experience. Its bodily systems fire up again, its mind relaxes and it returns to growth state.

With this great, organic pendulum swinging between states, we must still spend the majority of our time in growth, if we are to meet our fundamental human needs and reap the rewards of doing so. In general, however, people living in the Human Laboratory are not swinging healthily between protection and growth. Instead, they're sitting, crumpled up, inhaling and ingesting protection-enhancing toxins into their personal Petri dish. This is where the key to modern thriving lies.

To understand how to navigate from protection to growth in our demanding modern lives, we must learn to differentiate between toxins and nourishment. I do this by considering my **cells, microbiome and energy** and using nature as my filter to help best nourish those three parts of me.

As foraging, foresting, hunting and gathering beings, we had a vast understanding of foods that were toxic and others that were growth-promoting. Think fungi! There are toxic mushrooms that may seriously harm you. There are mushrooms that will nourish you and enhance growth and there are 'illegal' yet medicinal mushrooms that are now being used to heal depression. Apply this template to crops, vegetables and fruit grown organically in biodiverse-rich, fungal and microbial soils. Now consider their equivalents grown in depleted, degraded, pesticide dirt, to be processed to give them a long shelf life and fortified due to nutrient deficiency – the zoo foods that end up in brightly attractive packaging with an insane amount of unknowable additives.

Based on Bruce Lipton's conclusions regarding the brain being an activator of our cell membranes and how they behave, positive emotions such as happiness, gratitude, kindness and love that instil presence and feelings of comfort and safety should be able to stimulate growth. While increasingly recognized in society as good for our mental health, this idea of positivity cannot be actualized by walking around all day chanting, 'I'm happy, I'm happy, I'm happy.'

If you have the time and discipline to continually cite positive affirmations, that's great. Most of us do not, nor should we have to. Ultimately, wellbeing must be a baseline, easy state, not a constant striving achieved only through repetition, habit, mantra. It is within the state of growth that the capacity for actual, real, long-term happiness lies.

Wellbeing is when you are in growth mono mode. The habits and habitats we choose should create that state for us. Once you can authentically feel, 'I'm happy', you're automatically in a state of growth.

I am being a human being, not a human doing. I am feeding my Petri dish with growth-promoting, high-vibrational, natural foods, grown on growth-promoting, high-vibrational soils and drinking natural water.

Which diet are you?

So far I have dragged you into this chapter on eating without even describing what 'eating like a Tony' means for me, personally? I'm guessing that you're looking for me to suggest the ideal diet. The thing is, we can apply any diet to this conversation, be that low-fat, low-carb, paleo, primal, veganism, vegetarianism, flexitarian. Are your shelves bursting with diet and cookery books, in which the authors claim to know what you, personally, need to eat? I've been there myself. I've gone from my parents' experimental, processed zoo foods of the 1980s, to the bodybuilder protein shakes for breakfast, lunch and dinner of the 1990s, to the Atkins and South Beach diets of the noughties, to the primal and paleo, to vegan and raw, to rainbows and bulletproof unicorns of more recent times. I've read the books and crunched my way through recipes for many years.

Like every other dietary label, the subject of paleo is vast, along with veganism, vegetarianism, keto, carnivore, flexitarian and whatever else has filtered into the mainstream. Paleo diet books, supplements and greens are all flying off the shelves. But the point is, Paleolithic woman/man was part of the ecosystem and not separate from it. If we are really going to think of identifying ourselves as a particular dietary label, then we have to go back and look more deeply at the evolution of the human diet – from primate to zoo human. This is where the 'Eat like a Tony diet' begins. Better still let's call it the 'Be More Human' diet. Always access your nutrition with this question in mind: Is it good for the human and good for the environment?

By turning away from our processed zoo foods and mono-cropped farmed cereal grains and instead tuning back into the hunter-gatherer mindset, I feed my microbiome and cells and increase mitochondria function. Where possible I choose between regenerative, biodynamic and organic farming for my veggies, with the understanding that these are about healing the microbial soils. Thinking back to my conversation with Abby Rose, communication between the plant and the soil means that my veggies receive what they need through the soils and so do I, which in turn feeds my microbiome, cells, mitochondria and my mood, too.

Looking at the evidence from Terry Wahls around omega 6, grain-fed and antibiotic-fed animals; at Weston Price's links between processed foods, mouth breathing and dental problems; at the microbiome studies of indigenous tribes that have been eating the same way for thousands of years – I'd be hard pushed to want to consume a monocropped, grain-fed, processed zoo diet that compromised my digestion, my cells and my mitochondria. My 'rules' are simple:

- If you are eating meat, don't eat meat that comes from a domesticated, depressed, antibiotic-pumped animal that has been fed on pesticide-sprayed, monocropped grain.
- And if you're not eating meat, don't *become* a domesticated, depressed animal fed on antibiotics and pesticide-sprayed inflammatory grains and monocrops. Avoid the industrial, fake and processed farmed zoo foods.

When you take the opportunity to rewild your eating and drinking, you'll start to gain back some of those more intuitive food nudges yourself, just like the Viking. But surely it's time to get beyond the diet label. How do you define your eating habit? Carnivore? Vegan? Paleo? Keto? Vegetarian? Labels like these drive statements like 'vegan is good' or 'paleo is bad' and leave no room for us to feel into our human needs. Both the vegan and paleo communities feel very strongly that these are much more than dietary labels; they are lifestyles, not just a diet. Divisive labelling is also 'digestive disabling' – the more stressed we become, the less likely it is for our wild digestive system to be firing. When factoring in geographic locations and seasons, this makes absolutely no sense, let alone all the dynamics of your evolution. They can lead to an inorganic relationship with foods and the environment, which leads to us becoming dismissive of our true needs.

Psychological stress ramps up our desire for highly palatable (sweet, salty, fatty) zoo foods, which influences our microbiome, leading to further dysbiosis. As soon as those stress hormones enter the digestive tract, they literally reshape the gut bacteria, altering our mood, causing depression and deeper anxiety . . . and from here, we keep feeding the beast. **Your mood affects your gut and your gut affects your mood.**

I choose to eat foods that are good for the human and good for the environment – natural, fresh foods in their natural form from the best natural source I can find. Foods that are free from zoo dairy, gluten and refined sugar; in their whole state, either wild, organic or biodynamic. Foods that are raw or cooked lovingly, respectfully and carefully, to keep as many nutrients as possible intact. All to rewild my gut garden and spread the wealth of diversity from beneath the ground to my ground living table and my thriving Tony cells.

So, if anyone asks whether I'm vegan, low fat, keto, low carb, paleo or vegetarian, I reply that, through fasting and applying nature as a filter through the evolution of our human diet and by removing the labels, dogmas and expectations inhibiting me from tuning in to make the appropriate self-medicating decisions around food for my human needs, I eat like an intuitive Tony.

What's in your water?

Tap water contains myriad different chemicals including chlorine and fluoride – and pharmaceutical medications are showing up in tap water as well. Hormones, heavy metals, plastic and pollution can all make their way into what we drink. If I introduce those to my Petri dish, what is the outcome? That's right, put toxins in and my cells will behave in a protection state.

The average adult human body is made up of 50–65% water, making this element vital for every aspect of life. Which prompts the question: How important is the quality of this predominant element?

We all know that water is an integral element for keeping us alive and helping us feel our best. We drink it, we bathe in it; clean, toxin-free water is one of our fundamental needs. With pure water, you can add more nourishment to your urban environment (see page 152).

Rewilding your palate

Having previously introduced fasting and tech to the evolutionary table, I found it incredibly useful for rewilding my palate. I used home stool-sample testing to understand my microbiome and blood work to analyse what my cells needed, enabling me to discover how to eat for my Tony cells and my Tony bacteria. This meant I had a list of foods to minimize or remove that weren't supporting my growth and that I simply couldn't assimilate, or that were setting me up for gut dysbiosis and future inflammatory diseases, leading to a lack of energy and triggering negative emotions. But it wasn't all doom and gloom. My microbiome testing also provided me with a great template of what foods I could maximize and eat in abundance, what foods were my superfoods and what I could eat occasionally. The microbiome test provided me with a list of probiotics which would help nourish 'Tony's' microbiome, therefore further enabling my symbiotic gut to support my overall well-being. This process, alongside fasting, using breathwork and removing zoo processed foods, provides a great template for the 'Be More Human' diet.

I dismantled the old inherited templates of how I believed my plate should look and, more importantly, of how my microbiome, mitochondria and cells should be not only surviving, but thriving. Through this process, I removed the guessing game and the misinformation from fad diets. I once had someone trying to persuade me to pursue the rainbow diet, but I'd already tested for what I knew instinctively – that I was allergic to the nightshade family of plants. So, that put red, yellow and green peppers, red and yellow tomatoes and purple aubergines out of the equation. For me, rainbow eating isn't the best way! The message to myself was, 'You need to become empowered by what foods *a Tony needs.*' And this should be your message to yourself, too.

Steps to rewilding your eating and drinking

It's crucial to your survival to have your digestive system in good working order. If that's out of whack, you might find that you're overfed, but undernourished. Here are some exercises to digest.

EAT INTUITIVELY

Down-regulation and fasting are key to becoming consciously aware of your food choices and establishing a healthy mind and body relationship with food.

- Take a moment to breathe, deconstruct and step back from your inherited food templates, be that your own pacifying wants or peer pressure from your circle of friends.
- Establish what your own human needs are. With the mind of a beginner and a receptive belly, explore the organic vs inorganic food realms.

- Try a zoo food fasting move by cutting all the CRAP (**C**hemicals, **R**efined sugar and flour, **A**rtificial colours, sweeteners and flavouring, **P**rocessed products) from your diet for 72 hours. Journal the experience to see whether these foods have a hold on you emotionally.

EAT SEASONAL, EAT LOCAL

Eating with the seasons is a better choice for humans as well as for the environment (provided your seasonal foods are grown organically and free from pesticides). If you can't survive on it without destroying whole ecosystems, and shipping it from one continent to another, then you should really be asking yourself some questions.

- Build a conscious relationship with your food, your community and your local environment – connecting with the farmers and origins of the foods, knowing the paths the food has taken from the source – be that wild, organically farmed or gardened – and how they have arrived at your door.
- Become what you feed your mind and body – from the food you consume to the communities and environments you immerse in and absorb. If you have the space you can always up your game and grow your own, building a relationship with the soils and what is grown in those soils – it doesn't get any more seasonal or local than this.

MUNCH MINDFULLY

Being consciously aware of how you receive food is extremely important. It's not just inorganic food we want to avoid, it's inorganic behaviour around food, too. It's really quite difficult to ignite your wild sensory signals of smell, sight, texture, taste if you're chowing down in an up-regulated, typing-and-swiping feeding mindset. Just as much as the organic plate you're eyeing up through your belly, your environment will influence the nutrient absorption and how you feel.

- Be present, setting up yourself and your environment for optimal absorption.
- Try this Riddle Tribe practice: relax your lower abdomen (belly), then take a long inhale, hold, exhale and give thanks to the kingdoms of foods that we are about to receive – think grace and gratitude and treat your food as sacred.

EAT WELL ON THE MOVE

Sometimes, we have to eat on the move. The hunter-gatherers did (they had their name for a reason).

- Despite only ever being advised to sit down to eat by the socially normal police – which isn't the natural normal way at all – I prescribe that you breathe down into your belly and walk mindfully.
- Drop the walking pace by 10%, breathe deep and preferably get off the grey linear streets; drop into some lush nature, even find a more tree-lined street if a park or green space isn't available.

FORAGE FOR YOUR FARE

Foraging is the ultimate mindful practice that reconnects us to the all-important communication between the soil, our food and our belly. It's a feast for the sensory gains where we feed and nourish *all* our senses.

- Only pick what you are familiar with. I recommend doing your research to find five things to which you can confidently say 'Yes, I can definitely eat this.' And, once confident, find the next five plants to familiarize yourself with.
- Download a foraging app for identifying plants. There are some great options for mushroom picking, too. You simply take a photo of the plant and wait for the growth-promoting thumbs up or the toxic this-is-a-no-go. Use tech until, over time, you refine your own skill.

DIGEST DEEPLY

Rather than the amount of kombucha, kimchi or probiotic you guzzle, it's your emotional being and the environment that you choose to be at one with that will determine how and if you digest. With the Hadza tribe, it's their environment and whole lifestyle – as well as their diet – that influence their phenomenal gut health. Movement, sleep, rest, food, breathing, sunlight, soils, human connection and their life of inconvenience – all lead to such resilience.

- Aim to up your own elemental nutrition and grounding practices. Getting sunlight and fresh air will drop you into a down-regulated digester.
- The more organic, natural and wild your food, the better for our naturally diverse microbiome and symbiotic gut. Unless you want dysbiosis, I'd recommend avoiding these zoo foods: inorganic veg, poor vegetable oils, processed meats (including fake meat), refined sugars, grain (including grain-fed animals), pesticide-fed monocrops, antibiotics (including antibiotic-fed meat).

POOP PROPERLY

Indigenous people have more pooping prowess. They're primed for digestion, with their down-regulated parasympathetic state, a much higher fibre intake, more diverse microbiome and natural pooping position, AKA the squat. Traditional naturopaths, including Hippocrates, the father of natural medicine, believed the number of poops per day should be between two and three, which is more in line with what is seen in traditional cultures. Researchers have also reported vast variations in stool volume around the world. In Sweden and England, people pooped an average 150 grams per day. Top of the charts was Uganda, with an enviable pooping volume of 470g per day.

- Down-regulate your breath, slow down the pace of all that you do by 10%.
- Get the tech off the table when you're eating, turn notifications off and chew more.
- Feed your biome by feasting on more plants.
- Squat on the pot.

DOWN-REGULATE THROUGH BETTER BREATHING

As much as becoming a *breatharian* moments before each meal would help you to down-regulate and return to a state of rest-and-digest, not everyone wants or is able to reach that level of consciousness.

- I recommend down-regulating through better breathing, as you won't be making emotional decisions about the food you eat.
- Paying attention to your breath will help you navigate your food pathway more intuitively, so that you focus on 'digestion' and 'absorption' – your human needs over your human wants.

BECOME WATER

Rather than just drinking water or even bathing in it, think what water you want to *become*. What we drink, bathe in, are pool-birthed in and built from – it matters.

- Choose clean, toxin-free water. While natural spring water is best, if it's being stripped and shipped from its natural habitat to arrive in our supermarket aisle, and presented in plastic bottles, we have to question how good this is for us in the long term.
- Try a tap water fast. It's only when you stop drinking tap water that you really notice how much it reeks of chlorine.
- Tap water contains a long list of not-so-natural unsavouries that will contribute to the 50–60% watery you. The way to flip this is to install a water filter that not only strips out the nasties, but restores your water back to its mineralized glory. In addition, I'd recommend purchasing a kitchen countertop vortex; this spins your water, reactivating those spring-water vibes.

NEXT » SLEEPING AND RESTING

- See all revealed about the 8-hour sleeping myth.
- Learn how to get your best dose of melatonin.
- Find out how to rewild your sleeping environment.

CHAPTER 7

Sleeping and Resting

Sleep is one of the most fundamental of the biologically normal human needs. I have had people attend my retreats and, after taking one look at them, have told them to skip the full rewilding programme and just stay in bed and surrender to sleep. To me, this is the most important aspect to healing the self: rest and sleep, sleep and rest. Sleep is the great, ultimate connecter to our growth state. It is in sleep and in good sleep hygiene that the anabolic (growth) rebuilding of our 40-plus trillion cells can occur.

Media reports tell us we're living in the middle of a sleep deprivation endemic. We're actually living in an endemic of toxicity: noise and air pollution, toxic information, thermogenic dysfunction, electromagnetic field pollution – all are poor sleep habitat factors. But it's light pollution from switching on at sunset and all our night-time typing and swiping that truly inhibits the release of a hormone called melatonin, while maintaining levels of dopamine. It's a cacophony of disruption for our primordially wired bodies, which want to switch hormones on and off at the appropriate time of day and night. In this chapter we'll be looking more closely at melatonin, as well as how to make light and dark work for us.

Here's some good news. Not only can we prevent further damage to our intricate hormonal systems by quitting the night light, we can, in fact, reverse the effects of any disruption already caused! Mice administered with melatonin after the removal of their pineal gland, without any other change to their environments, lost weight – an occurrence also known to be possible in humans who experience excessive exposure to blue light and those who work night shifts. (More on this later.)

Sleep changes our genetic expression and supports immune and hormonal system function, renal health, cardiac function, blood pressure, stress levels, adrenal function, thyroid and gastrointestinal health . . . but only within an environment which honours a natural sleep.

I'd been obsessed with getting enough sleep, just like anyone else. When I first arrived at sleep as being one of the fundamental human needs that must be met before we can achieve total wellbeing, the numerous studies left me scratching my ginger Nordic-Celtic beard. The dictatorial advice of sleep's popular advocates put a look of chimp-like puzzlement on my face. Something wasn't right in the common advice being dished out.

It was some time before I began to understand the science behind sleep and how it has worked in nature for hundreds of thousands of years. I discovered what happens when we remove the environmental toxins that disrupt our sleep cycles and block true, anabolic (regenerative) sleep. Contrary to what many other health practitioners and sleep experts say, I suggest that our fixation with sleep is misplaced. Sleep is fundamentally important to regaining and maintaining natural health, absolutely. But it is, in fact, the quality of our sleep habitat that dictates its positive effects on our health, not the number of hours we habitually clock up in slumberland.

I'm going to show you why I don't buy into the mainstream zoo human science around sleep, by breaking down the realities of how sleep works in nature for us as a natural species. Let me demonstrate why, as long as you get your hormones doing their jobs properly, you can forget all about that 8-hour target and rid yourself of myriad sleep debt ills.

Now here's a caveat. You can have every other one of my Be More Human protocols in place, with your food choices nailed and your digestion running smoothly. You can move like Mowgli, be drinking natural spring water, breathing clear air, burying your bare feet down in the earth, inhaling those aromatic terpenes, interacting safely with the sun and vibing with your tribe of influence. But it is only when you're getting regular, natural, anabolic sleep that you're able to unite all of these elements. Sleep is the glue that sticks together all of your other nature gains to build the best, thriving version of you.

Going back to the garden

Let's travel back to a time well before the genesis of the Human Laboratory, millennia before any human could dream up such an invention as the light bulb or have any need for a light bulb moment. Let your urban home, the buildings rising in all directions around you, the traffic and pavements and billboards, melt into the earth. Dismantle the plumbing and sewer systems and the electricity boards, dissolve the smog and fumes, extinguish the light pollution. Take off your shoes, and your clothes, while you're at it. Remove your television, your laptop and your smartphone from existence. Take away your central heating. Disconnect your WiFi. Completely deconstruct the environment in which you're currently living. In its place, begin to conjure up the ancient landscape of primitive humans. Allow trees and plants to spring up from the boundless fertile soils and grass beneath your bare feet. Let in animals, insects and predators to share your surroundings freely. Appreciate how the panorama is composed simply of vegetation, fresh water sources, an uninterrupted horizon and expansive sky.

You are now living in a time when the only light that can filter into your eyeballs is of natural origin – sunlight, moonlight, starlight – and the light from our own human discovery, fire. Feel yourself tuning in to the subtle fluctuations in temperature, as you hunt for your food. You know that your time is structured according to the natural cycles of day and night. You live here now, in this simple, stripped-back environment. This is your tech-free, chair-less, pre-electromagnetic field (EMF) home.

Dusk is setting in. You must gather up some dry stones and spark up a fire to keep yourself and your tribe warm and calm. As the sun bows to the moon, the night air cools and you move in closer to your tribe members to snuggle down and keep warm while the fire burns on.

Before the Human Laboratory, before we entered this current age of chronic disconnection, which has left us barely able to offer more contact to our fellow race members than the occasional, swift nod of thanks when somebody offers us their seat on the train, humans used to partake in frequent group cuddle sessions – for real! During the night, you take turns with your tribe members to feed the fire, keeping it roaring just enough so its multipurpose-serving heat will remain for when morning arrives.

A new day announces its arrival with the beauteous break of the early sun illuminating the earth and a warm glow begins to creep towards your resting place. Rising temperature prompts the start of your waking day and you're roused to watch the rest of the sunrise. Growing daylight begins to stimulate your brain, just enough to instigate some happiness-promoting hormone action and stir your metabolism. The temperature is still cool, so you start your natural movement and mobility session early. (Just kidding, we obviously didn't need dedicated classes at this point in time – we simply moved around exactly how nature intended us to and maintained lean physiques, functional muscles and healthy cardiovascular systems just fine!)

Now, let's remove you from your ancestral habitat, where you may well feel rested and primed for what your body needs you to perform that day, and return you to the familiar surroundings of your urban home. Perhaps you'll be able to gain a fresh perception on your night-time and morning routines.

Back to your daily routine

Early evening. You've arrived home from a manic day at work, possibly after a couple of post-work drinks and a trip on the Tube, or some time stuck in traffic. Instead of falling asleep by the light of the moon and fire, you are wide-eyed, swiping and typing into the light of your smartphone. Perhaps the television is also on in the background, Netflix episodes streaming into your subconscious. The unforgiving overhead light is on, possibly the central heating is cranked up. When you eventually decide to prise your eyes from your screen and nod off, the street light outside seeps through the gap around your blinds, the traffic rumbles on behind the window and your phone remains connected to the big grid, alert, receiving, transmitting next to your head. When you wake in the night to use the toilet, you switch the bathroom light on without even thinking, momentarily blasting blue spectrum light into the eyes of your half-awake body.

Before morning has even officially begun in your biological world, outside the sky is still dark, the chide of your alarm crashes into your unconsciousness, disorientating you, nagging you to rush to your commute. The sudden wake is almost painful, though, so you tap snooze – almost subconsciously – and prepare to face the jarring alarm and feelings of disgruntled anger again in eight minutes' time. But not before you've gazed, eyes half open to the blackness of early morning around you, into your phone's screen, checking in on the notifications you received overnight.

When you consider our modern lives this way, it's not surprising we're all walking around groggy, grumpy, in need of caffeinating and with our hormones, digestion and immune system all askew. Sure, we may have come a long way technologically as a species, but our bodies remain primal – especially where sleep is concerned. Your body may be incredibly smart but it still cannot tell the difference between being woken by a predator and the daily call that signals work. So, the question: what was the primary driver of change here? Between this picture of wild sleep dictated by nature and our modern night-time routine? And our resulting relationship with night and day, light and dark? The light bulb. The lighting we have installed in our homes emits a blue and green spectrum of light which acts as a sinister saboteur of our sleep – it categorically does not work in nature. The conventional light bulb is responsible for flooding our rooms, our eyeballs and the cells of our skin with sleep-disrupting blue light. The bulb in your ceiling is but one rogue in a whole team of tricksters we have illuminated our environments with, under the belief they are improving our lives. Our televisions, smartphones, computer screens and street lamps are all emitting blue light, forcing important hormones into hiding, as our brains recognize this light as daylight.

The reason why illuminating our cities, public transport and houses with artificial blue light in the evening is of such great detriment to our sleep is primarily down to the way it all affects melatonin. This hormone is needed to attain growth-promoting, disease-preventing, deep sleep. Here's the kicker, though: melatonin is linked up to our ancient circadian rhythms and is therefore only released into the body when we're in *biological darkness*. The blue light we bathe in every night directly inhibits its release. This subsequent lack of melatonin results in a disruptive chemical cascade that can lead to a plethora of cellular and digestive issues and diseases, hormonal imbalance, infertility, mood disorders and compromised immune health. Much more of that later. Right now, I want to take you back to nature.

Tribal truths

Evidence-based science is coming in thick and fast to confirm the intricate and disruptive relationship between artificial light and sleep. But what really does help is to see the flip side of its effects. To simultaneously debunk the 8-hour myth, we can turn to modern hunter-gatherer tribes who have been living the same way for thousands of years to show us how it's done the natural way.

You know by now that I have a rather large issue with the modern reductionist way of removing something from the symbiosis of nature and examining it in isolation in a laboratory, then presenting those results to make absolute claims on how we should live. When every element in nature is so intelligently designed to work as one ecosystem, removing one factor and expecting valuable data is a redundant method. This is where my problems with the general consensus around good sleep hygiene arise: the sleep studies which prompted the 8-hour conclusion were all conducted within the compromised environment of the Human Laboratory itself. Return to nature and observe biologically natural sleeping patterns in conjunction with these studies, however, and we arrive at an altogether different conclusion.

The great J. Krishnamurti stated that it is no measure of health to be well adjusted to a profoundly sick society. I think it is no measure of health and wellbeing to be well adjusted to a profoundly sick environment.

Some incredible sleep studies conducted outside of the Human Laboratory show us how nature herself intended our night-time habits and habitats to work. As it transpires, our tribal brothers and sisters aren't descending into uninterrupted slumber for 8 solid hours from sunset to sunrise. And when you think about it, it makes sense. If it was natural for humans to sleep in such a way, we wouldn't be here today! In hostile environments, when sleeping means increased vulnerability through having your defences down against predators, rival tribes and the natural elements, it would work against our survival to be unconscious for such an extended period of time.

Studying natural sleep

Jerome Siegel, from the University of California, visited three pre-industrialized modern tribes to observe Homo sapiens' sleep patterns from an uncompromised, biologically normal perspective. The study group was comprised of 94 volunteers and 1,165 days' worth of data across the three groups of tribespeople from three separate geographical locations: the Hadza hunter-gatherers of Tanzania, the San hunter-gatherers of Namibia and the Tsimané hunter-agriculturists of Bolivia.

The three semi-nomadic tribes live mostly outside in close-knit groups, without electricity, heating and cooling systems, modern medicine and the modern-day media distractions so often accused of disrupting our natural sleep patterns; they therefore offer the most biologically normal means of studying Homo sapiens as it is possible to get.

Looking at the findings, all three groups showed similar sleep patterns, suggesting that a natural baseline state exists for human sleep organization, regardless of geographical location. The sleep pattern of the groups was also shown to be strongly regulated by the seasons, with the volunteers averaging 53–56 minutes longer time asleep in the winter, coincident with a 1.2-hour increase in the San and 2-hour increase in the Tsimané tribes during winter.

The average time for falling asleep was more than 3 hours after sunset and wake time was usually pre-dawn, abolishing the supposition of many modern paleo communities that we should be asleep during all hours of darkness. Although the tribespeople woke at the same time each day, with daily variability between the waking time of individuals almost non-existent, it wasn't light cycles that determined wake and sleep times, but temperature fluctuations. None of the tribal volunteers reported incidences of insomnia. In fact, two of the tribes didn't even have a word for it in their respective languages!

Upon 220 hours of observation of 33 participants of the Hadza tribe of Tanzania, there were just 18 minutes where every tribe member was asleep at the same time. A third of the group on average was alert, or lightly dozing, at any given time and members of the group rose up to several times during the night to look after the young, tend to the fire, smoke and use the toilet. Some members fell asleep as early as 10pm, woke lightly throughout the night and then woke around 6am, while others stayed up past 11pm and got up after 8am. Daytime napping occurred on 7% of days in winter and less than 22% of days in summer.

Siegel was able to establish that, running on 5.7–7.1 hours of sleep per night, hunter-gatherers do not sleep for 8 hours, or for longer than we do in the industrialized world. So, while we berate ourselves for not clocking up at least 8 hours each night, it turns out our ancestors weren't, and our contemporary biological relations aren't either.

The fact that there has been no reported seasonal effect on sleep duration within urban societies suggests that our dissociation from nature is even more nuanced and significant than we realized. Not only is our innate biology contending with the modern dismantling of our melatonin production, but due to our insulated, heated, air-conditioned modern housing, it is suffering from the adverse effects of no longer being guided in and out of sleep by our thermogenic response to the natural rising and falling of our environmental temperature. It's better to have fewer hours of good-quality sleep at night, uncompromised by the modern environment, than 8 hours of sleep with suppressed melatonin levels and tinkered-with room temperature.

Do you get 8 hours' sleep at night and still find yourself flagging in the afternoons? Despite their active daytimes of hunting and gathering, our tribal relatives experience no such need for naps halfway through the day. The 3pm slump is an urbanite phenomenon!

While 10–30% of people in industrialized society are suffering from insomnia, the tribespeople were not sleeping solidly from dusk till dawn, nor napping during the day. Yet they are in excellent, biologically normal health.

The tribespeople's average lifespan is relatively low compared to us here in the Human Zoo, but this is due to infant mortality, death in childbirth, death by wild animals, infection and accidental death, rather than from chronic disease, stress-related chronic conditions and lifestyle factors. They live virtually disease-free and their collective BMI falls within the normal range. Blood pressure is low and there is zero presence of risk factors for cardiovascular disease. The Tsimané, who are hunter-agriculturalists, have higher physical fitness than industrial populations and many are living this way into their sixties, seventies, eighties and beyond.

Our hunter-gatherer brothers and sisters are surviving out in the wild, hunting for food, exposed to the elements and always vulnerable to predators. And they're definitely not sleeping for 8 hours every night. Remember that these hunter-gatherer tribes are in a rest-and-digest, down-regulated, parasympathetic state. If you spend the majority of your day in this state, then you are operating from the system nature intended for you, so the need to remove yourself to take a power nap or to take a moment out to rest your eyes isn't necessary.

Likewise, the tribes aren't experiencing air pollution, noise pollution, light pollution or absorbing the toxic news at ten before bed;

they breathe clean air, the sun has dropped and the only sounds are that of the natural world. Instead of the TV or smartphone, they have fireside chats. The Instagram world of comparison only serves to bring us into our up-regulated stressed-out state.

Each of the tribal groups were waking before sunrise, which straight away contrasts with the wake-time of Westerners, who typically wake when it's light. The volunteers obtained their most light exposure at around 9am and retreated to the shade at midday when the sun is strongest. The three tribal groups often had small fires alight and would have been exposed to the light of the moon and stars, but the light levels within their sleep spaces remained low. The daily reduction in light is followed by the daily reduction in temperature.

'It is absolutely incorrect,' Siegel stated upon conclusion of his study, 'that the more you sleep the healthier you'll be.' So why have we developed an apparent need to slumber for so much longer than our biology requires?

The eight-hour myth

It is now universally acknowledged that we need 7–9 hours' (an average of 8 hours) sleep each night to maintain good health. This number is taken as gospel and individuals all over the Western world are shooting for this magic number of hours in bed each night, feeling triumphant when they hit it, guilty when they don't. And probably still not functioning at their physical or emotional best even if they do. Not only do we have the pressure of the 8-hour mark to adhere to, but we are also contending with the purported looming health consequences of 'sleep debt' for every night we fall short. Matthew Walker, author of *Why We Sleep*, writes: 'If I were to take a human being and deprive them of sleep for one night, so that they've lost eight hours of sleep and then I give them all of the recovery sleep that they want on a second, a third, even a fourth night, they do sleep longer but they never get back that full eight hours that they've lost . . . Mother Nature has never had to face the challenge of sleep deprivation during the course of evolution and therefore, she's never had to come up with a safety net mechanism that overcomes a sleep debt.'

While it's helpful to establish a sleep goal to strive for, the downside could be that reaching that target becomes another source of stress. For many people, 8 hours isn't practical – particularly when you run a business, have a busy commute or a young family. What if you don't achieve your 8 hours?

To better understand the inherent health benefits of natural lighting, we're going to take a deep dive into the world of our hormonal systems to visit the hormone I like to call 'sleep's superfood'. As the tribespeople show, the delayed melatonin response to darkness is adaptive in facilitating sleep after darkness, bringing the entire sleep period in synchrony with the lowest night-time temperatures.

MELATONIN — THE SCIENCE BEHIND OUR SUPERHORMONE

Melatonin works synergistically with other hormones to keep the incredible biological machine of the human body working as it should. It's a vastly undervalued powerhouse . . .

- Acts as scavenger molecule, anti-inflammatory and antioxidant, reducing oxidative stress from toxins.

- Controls metabolism, with anti-obesity, anti-ageing and anti-cancer properties.
- Regulates the immune system and carcinogenic processes.
- Controls reproductive functions and affects mood, including depression and Seasonal Affective Disorder.
- Helps eye function, protecting against radiation and controlling many cellular processes, including the synthesis of important molecules.

Melatonin influences our sleep patterns and the quality of our sleep. Its production increases during the night and decreases during the daytime when we're exposed to light. It works synergistically with our circadian rhythm and with darkness.

We can identify a direct link between melatonin and obesity – a precursor to metabolic disorders, from type 2 diabetes and cancers including breast cancer to cardiovascular disease. Obesity and being overweight can now be observed as conditions evident right across the Western world and that the hormone may have control over blood glucose, lipid and cholesterol levels is becoming well evidenced. Empowering information is now emerging that could indicate that the key to health is a lot simpler than we think.

A study published in the journal *Diabetes, Metabolic Syndrome and Obesity: Targets and Therapy* showed an improvement in the sleep of insomniac type 2 diabetics and regulation of their blood glucose levels after 3 weeks and 5 months, respectively, of melatonin supplementation. Similarly, the *Journal of Pineal Research* published data in 2011 that showed patients with metabolic issues measured lower cholesterol and blood pressure after 2 months of melatonin supplementation. Additional tests performed on type 1 and type 2 diabetic mice showed that melatonin supplementation helped to regulate metabolism during activity and rest, improved insulin action and helped to regulate fat intake and metabolism. (None of this means that you should be taking a melatonin supplement! Doing this can be significantly detrimental to many biological factors, including insulin, depending on dosage and the timing it is administered. I'm merely showing you the research here. At the end of the chapter I'll give you all the practical advice you need to get your own dose.)

A physiologist at the University of São Paulo, José Cipolla Neto, conducted research on the relationship between melatonin and obesity and concluded: 'Our data confirms the importance of melatonin for the control of food intake, energy expenditure by the organism, and the storage of energy at sites such as adipose tissue and the liver. We can say that melatonin plays a fundamental role in regulating body weight.'

Melatonin is a proven anti-diabetes, anti-weight gain, pro-insulin hormone. The hormone's influence on these areas of physiology has been attributed to its job controlling the synchronization of energy metabolism as it fluctuates naturally during the day. That is, it is a fundamental chronobiotic, meaning that it regulates circadian rhythm. At relatively specific times of day, we wake up, expend energy while moving around our environment in daily activities and input energy from food. Other times, we rest and make use of stored energy. Melatonin is the regulator of this energy balance and metabolism. When melatonin is suppressed, insulin and this circadian rhythm become dysregulated.

Get into your circadian rhythm

Melatonin is regulated by the pineal gland, found in the brain. The pineal gland has a somewhat mystical association thanks to being the last gland of the endocrine system to be discovered. It is often referred to as the 'third eye', due to its intricate relationship with light and its location deep inside the brain. This controls your circadian rhythm – the 24-hour biological cycle, or 'biological clock', of sleep–wake patterns dictated by daylight and darkness.

To explore the importance of melatonin in these systems, Cipolla Neto and his team removed the pineal glands of a group of mice in order to cease their melatonin production. Two months later, without melatonin in their systems and with no change in their diets or lifestyles, the mice presented with metabolic disorders, including hypertension, insulin resistance and early development of obesity. They also showed higher than normal sugar (glucose) and fat (lipid) levels in their blood, resulting in fat storage in white adipose tissue and in the liver. Mice groups administered with melatonin directly after having their pineal glands removed showed no signs of metabolic disturbance. Of equal importance when it comes to managing the incline of modern chronic conditions naturally, the mice also began consuming more food than they did before being separated from their pineal glands. Not only were they doing so at irregular and abnormal times, they were expending less energy on account of their raised glucose and lipid levels. The study also highlighted that, following removal of the pineal gland, the mice lost the positive metabolic adaptations usually induced by exercise when melatonin is present.

Low levels of melatonin have been shown to directly stimulate the hypothalamic centres that instigate increased appetite, reduce the beneficial effects of exercise and drive up the amount of the 'hunger hormone' ghrelin in the blood. This has an influence on weight gain: high levels of melatonin, which occur naturally at night, act directly on a region of the brain called the hypothalamus, to inhibit hunger. Less melatonin therefore results in increased appetite. Melatonin reduction also deregulates the release and action of insulin. With low melatonin levels, two of the brain's appetite regulators are lost and less energy is expended. Triple trouble for promoting the development of diabetes and obesity!

Now, how do we suppress our melatonin production in such a way as to instigate such metabolic disaster? *By exposing ourselves to blue light at night.* 'The most powerful factors contributing to obesity,' says Cipollo Neto, 'are unquestionably nocturnal light pollution and night-shift work.' He even goes as far as to say that he believes nocturnal lighting is one of the main contributors to the epidemic of obesity in modern society. Incredible, right?

Melatonin influences a number of our physiological functions, one of which is blood sugar control. Hormone receptors compatible with melatonin – signalling to the body that it is dark and therefore time to wind down – are not only found in the eyes and brain, but in the pancreas and pancreatic beta cells, too. Beta cells release insulin, which controls the amount of glucose in the blood. Significantly, when melatonin activates these receptors, a decrease in insulin is instigated.

As we don't naturally eat during sleeping hours, blocking insulin action helps keep blood sugar levels stable while sleeping and supplies the brain with regular glucose during the night.

These daily rises and falls, along with the secretion of melatonin, support the idea that they are regulated by the circadian system via melatonin. This influence on insulin secretion may have evolved as a protective mechanism against low blood sugar levels while we are asleep.

There's been some useful research on sleep debt symptoms with shift workers, in whom rates of diabetes and obesity are rife. Night-shift workers demonstrate high glucose responses after meals. Their sleep schedules are artificially shifted from their natural circadian rhythms, therefore altering the natural patterns of their natural light exposure over 24 hours. Their lifestyles promote low melatonin levels, disrupting their long-term health.

Let's consider the results from an experiment with three groups of shift workers run by Bruce Lipton, the American biologist noted for promoting the view that – overriding factors like genetics – it's our beliefs that control human biology.

- Group One simulates night-shift work under blue spectrums of light, i.e. standard daylight-mimicking lighting.
- Group Two's subjects are placed, unworking, into natural darkness.
- Group Three also simulates night-shift work, like Group One, but subjects wear amber glasses to block blue light and mimic biological darkness, the amber tones experienced by indigenous tribes around the evening fire.

The results? Group One produces no melatonin; Groups Two and Three both have equally high and optimal levels of melatonin.

While I'm not asking you to wear amber glasses, the research shows how you can reverse this negative influence for yourself and get your right dosage of melatonin at the right time. If you are getting the recommended number of hours of sleep each night but not releasing sufficient melatonin, you will not be reaping the healing, building rewards of our slumber.

It's all in the quality

Where lack of sleep is so often blamed for so many health conditions, we can clearly see that it's the quality of the sleep and our bedtime routines that are actually causing the trouble. To wind down, your body needs melatonin to be released. If you're typing and swiping under the buzz of artificial light, it's the dopamine response that's been triggered, a hormone that helps you stay awake, by maintaining nerve activity in your eyes. Dopamine is great for the morning. In fact, I promote its release with a good move around under the morning sky. As dopamine is known as the motivational molecule or the seeking hormone, however, it's not conducive to being immersed in the land of nod.

In a natural setting, melatonin levels typically rise in the evening, when cortisol levels are lowering, promoting sleep; they then peak during the night, then fall in the morning. As natural light (sunlight) increases, cortisol levels rise again and your body picks up the happy hormone serotonin, dumping melatonin out to encourage wakefulness.

An absence or reduction of melatonin in the body has been shown to directly promote so many poor health conditions. Here's the kicker, though – melatonin is only triggered for release by biological darkness. When I speak of biological darkness, I'm simply referring to the kind of darkness we would have experienced as hunter-gatherers – darkness which included firelight, moon and starlight and an absence of blue and green light spectrums. That's right, that artificial, blue light we're feeding our bodies with each and every night shuts off the release of melatonin. As darkness descends, melatonin is released into your bloodstream and cerebrospinal fluid, telling several organs that it's time to wind down for sleep, taking on the mammoth operation of cleaning up our cells and preparing us for that healing, nutritious sleep. While other factors such as stress, poor daylight exposure, smoking and shift work may cause low levels of melatonin at night, it's exposure to too much light at night that's the greatest saboteur. We can and must do something about that.

Rewild your environment for sleep

It was on the opening day of hosting my very first retreat that I reached the realization of the need to rewild the environment when it comes to modern sleep. This was my first foray into an experiential, immersive, tangible version of the concepts which inspired me so much. My first chance to be the change, in a position of influence to pass my message on to others.

The setting is the Isle of Wight. Our group is staying in the most incredible safari-style tents, on open land with inspiring panoramas and the ability to light big, open fires. As host, I have an opportunity to play with my current knowledge. I can explore how to successfully reintroduce aspects of the wild to the lifestyles of modern urbanites to better improve their health and happiness in everyday city life. Look around at the real mixture of participants showing up . . . city workers, personal trainers, coaches, students, actors, IT consultants . . . All are here to start their individual journeys and our collective foray into rewilding. Joe, who I come to dub 'the sleepless lawyer', is also part of this first tribe. From the very beginning, I take a particular interest in Joe . . . not only is he a new one-to-one client of mine, but I have also by this point learned much about adrenal fatigue and how often medicine

and law students are used as examples in research as being particu-
larly prone to developing the condition. Now, here before me is a classic
case. Joe is a city man. He loves his city environment and cannot quite
see the fascination with nature the rest of the group has. He spends
most of the first day of the retreat head down, shoulders caved, staring
into his iPhone, in the want (not need!) to constantly check in with the
office and to stay continually up to date with the World Cup results. I
joke that he is more connected to his mobile phone than to nature and
the universe.

Joe, somewhat unsurprisingly, has all the symptoms indicative of an
existence in the Human Laboratory. He is stressed up to his tired
eyeballs, inflamed, has a poor typing-and-swiping kind of quality of
movement. And he cannot sleep for shit. The lack of movement, the lazy
food choices, the slack digestion and the constant choosing of wireless
connectivity over nature connectivity can all be addressed later. It is
Joe's losing battle with sleep that not only bothers him the most, but
most interests me of all of his human experience. Then, on night three,
nature claims her humble victory over Joe's stubborn inability to prop-
erly zonk out. Not only is he suddenly able to hit the hay with more
depth and ease than he ever has before in his adult life, but I begin to
find him in daylight hours snoozing under the trees, akin to the way a
growing child pauses in his adventures to heed his natural impulses and
take a nap.

Overnight, Joe's previous fixation on the World Cup transforms into
a new-found fascination with the real world around him. He has a
brand-new team to support: his new tribe, interdependent symbiosis,
the team formed of his very own cells. And with that, he slowly, but
with all of the vulnerability and willingness necessary for success,
begins to fall in love with reconnecting to his ancestral self. Once Joe's
monkey – his inability to chill out and get his head down – has been

shaken from his back, leaving him free to fling open the floodgates firstly to real resting, and then to his wider rewilding, we are able to concentrate on the other areas of his modern lifestyle which have left him surviving instead of thriving. And indeed, many of these other issues begin to see huge improvements simply as a result of the introduction of proper sleep into Joe's life.

Joe was a quintessential victim of the Human Laboratory definition of 'success'. Engulfed by the lifestyle promoted by motivational speakers and the corporate world, which encourage people to go harder, faster, longer, he was primed to be taken in and knew no alternative. All this glamorization of the stressed, sick, angry and superficially 'successful' entrepreneurs telling us on motivational social media posts that we should be 'killing it'; that we'll get all the sleep we need when we are dead! Actually, the combination of late-night screen time, lack of self-awareness and 'kudos' for high-stress lifestyles will certainly lead to shorter lifespans for humans who fall prey to it. Contrary to this mainstream opinion that sleep is an obstacle to 'killing it', sleep is a *vital conduit to wellbeing.* For us equatorial apes who want to avoid early-onset ageing, disease, inflammation, obesity and a demeanour like an angry toddler past its bedtime, we need to get our sleep habits and sleep habitats in check! Joe did. The man who was my epitome of sleep disruption as a symptom of Human Laboratory influence eventually became my exemplar of the healing, transformative power of natural sleep.

So, what exactly was it that clicked for Joe, and for so many others that I coach through this process, that enabled him to break a lifetime of terrible sleep habits? Does everyone have to commit to a week off the grid with their bed in a tent to make friends with sleep? No. And as I've said earlier, you don't even need to push for more hours within your busy schedule to make extra room for it. But you do need to reconnect with nature. Time and time again through workshops and retreats and coaching one-to-ones, I see the undeniable potency that comes from getting up close and personal with nature. Or at least with making a conscious commitment to mimicking nature and constructing a natural sleep environment within our Human Lab.

Joe was never going to change his stressful job and overworked lifestyle. But he didn't have to. Switching up his environment and rebooting his sleep cycle was all it took. It enabled him to drift easily into growth-promoting slumber as a nightly expectation, rather than the occasional luxury. For Joe, it started with that simple act of removing himself from the hustle and bustle of his brightly lit city. To be dropped into the unforgiving darkness and true silence of night. Natural fire and clean air were enough to reconnect him to his natural sleep rhythm. But returning home from the retreat, back to his regular environment without making changes in his everyday routine, would have seen his new Be More Human sleep short-lived.

Joe realized he had some work to do once he was back home. He wanted to maintain his new-found, growth-promoting, energy-enhancing sleep routine. Once he experienced what rewilded sleep felt like, Joe was more than willing to make the necessary changes to make it his norm. Changing this pattern is not too difficult a feat once you have your routine in place. With your house set up in your favour, nature will take care of the rest. It just means introducing a few simple rewilding protocols to balance out all of the sleep-disrupting stimuli of our modern environments.

We all need to rewild our existing environment with nature to enable our biological needs to be met. The quality of our sleep is a by-product of our lifestyle, so accessing the best possible sleep means we have to change both our *perception* of our lifestyle and the *actual environment* in which we choose to live that lifestyle. If you lead a natural lifestyle, you will enjoy natural sleep. If you live in a compromised environment, you will have compromised sleep. But here's the key: if you live in a compromised environment but set up your home to mimic nature as closely as possible, then you will be able to enjoy natural sleep without having to move out of your urban home or even having to commit to a resetting retreat. This is achievable for anybody – in fact, it's your birthright.

Realize that you need to create a more conscious sleep-hygiene routine and habitat – which means more than just switching off the lights and turning off the News at Ten. You won't get away with sidling off to bed to scroll the depths of Facebook, bathing your eyeballs in blue light, inhaling neurotoxins. It will be useless to count sheep while your ever-expanding to-do list throbs through your head.

Enough isn't enough

Here's a paradox. After that initial observation of Joe over the course of the retreat, I came to believe that it is infinitely better to be 'killing it', as long as you're honouring biological darkness, temperature and air. As long as you're fostering happy hormones within your everyday environment. If you are in a rewilded sleep environment I would even prefer you to be staying up a little later and forgoing the advice to achieve a minimum of 8 hours in bed, than build a habit of sleeping for hours and hours within the unnatural, sleep-disrupting, stress-promoting habitat of the Human Laboratory. Yes, I'm telling you that you're allowed to sleep less and can do so without incurring the health penalties associated with sleep deprivation. With one unconditional requisite: you must rewild your sleep habitats.

If I haven't convinced you of it already, let me be clear: as the most critical foundation of our physical, social, spiritual and emotional health, sleep is the most valuable practice to master in all realms of wellbeing. It is also one of the least costly interventions for restoring one's own total wellness. We pass a whopping one third of our lives sleeping, yet spend so little time becoming skilled in and honouring this free form of wellness, wellbeing and health intervention. So, what can we conclude from all of this?

- It's not the number of hours we sleep that are important but the environment in which we do it.
- The hormonal disruption and subsequent illnesses that many experts put down to sleep time is actually attributable to the dysregulation of melatonin and body temperature, air quality and up-regulated overwhelm.
- The 8 hours we're shooting for in our industrialized world clearly aren't compensating for our toxic environments – because we're still walking around with the lifestyle-induced chronic conditions – diabetes, obesity, autoimmunity, etc. – that plentiful sleep is supposed to prevent.
- We really do grow into all-round better human beings by improving the quality of our time in bed; deep sleep is anabolic sleep and, when achieved, amazing things start to happen.

Change our perspective and re-piece the puzzle together, however, and suddenly the picture is obvious. These changes need to come in the way we are living in our compromised environments. Let's get in at the root of the issue, do it naturally, and stop allowing our melatonin production to be lowered in the first place. The answer to unlocking the panacea of sleep as the ultimate healer? Rewilding your sleep environment.

Steps to rewilding your sleep

Rewilding your sleep environment will pave the way for you to go deep, dark and thriving at night by regulating your melatonin levels, getting your indoor temperature optimal, and your air pure. Implement the steps below and make them a part of your rewilding routine. I promise you, it's worth it. You'll be richly rewarded with the best sleep – and all the benefits that come with it – for life.

GET THE BEDROOM BACK

Bedrooms are for reading, rest, sex and sleeping, not working or ranting on the phone.

• Keep the TV, typing, swiping and zooming outta the bedroom.

REDUCE THE TOXINS

Being bedroom-aware, we have to assess the wonderful blend of toxins we're exposed to when horizontal. Consider the paints, mastics, glues, soft furnishings, carpets in your bedroom, as well as the central heating that cooks everything.

• Access the NASA list for air-purifying plants that thrive at night and can help filter out a long list of neurotoxins, such as benzene, formaldehyde, trichloroethylene, xylene, toluene and ammonia.

ENHANCE THE AIR

Let's consider the air inside our sleep box, the room in which we spend a third of our lives inhaling the same experience. Do we want the air to be growth-promoting or compromising?

- Acquiring an air purifier will eliminate 99% of impurities in your giant grow bag, although I'd still recommend inviting some plants into the mix for that hit of nature in the senses.

SWITCH YOUR MATERIALS

Think about swapping out your materials from inorganic to organic, whether that's the bedding, your PJs, paints or upholstery. Bit by bit, make the organic shift.

- If you're going to use candles instead of circadian lighting for the shift to biological darkness, try tea lights and use jars to house the candles, for safety.

BLOCK OUT THE BLUE LIGHT

You can make a simple start to claiming your biological darkness at night. Buy a pair of amber shades to reduce your blue light exposure when commuting home late under the eye-watering glare of tube lighting.

- If you want to up your game in the melatonin growth stakes, you can install amber lighting throughout your home. Just switch regular light bulbs for circadian lighting – there are a number of brands to choose from.

LOWER THE TEMPERATURE

When the sun goes down, the temperature goes with it. Why not work with that?

- Instead of cranking up the heating, keep the bedroom cool to prime your night-time hormonal system.

CHOOSE YIN PRACTICES OVER YANG

Support your anabolic healing cycle by avoiding high-impact training after 6pm.

- Instead, choose mindful mobility and movement practices that are much more calming and grounding.

BE MINDFUL IN THE EVENING

In the evening, avoid the up-regulating toxic news or horror movies of butchery and madness and be mindful with your caffeine, sugar and alcohol intake.

- If you have to have the pacifying box on, tune into down-regulating romantic or funny movies.
- When it comes to socially acceptable drink and drugs of an evening, perhaps journal your timings with these to tune in and understand how these stimulating experiences impact your sleep cycle.

BREATHE TO DOWN-REGULATE

Drop into your parasympathetic, rest-and-digest, growth-promoting state.

- Choose one of the down-regulating breathing techniques from the Breathing and Being chapter.

USE LIGHT TO WAKE UP

Go deep enough into your thriving state from 10pm and you will eventually begin to wake naturally at the same time each day, without the need for artificial stimulation.

- Try a clock that brings you gently back into your wake state with gradual light, rather than the urbanite equivalent of the sabre-toothed tiger – your screaming alarm.

WAKE UP AT THE SAME TIME EACH DAY

Trigger all that dopamine, serotonin, melatonin and endorphins.

- Regardless of the night you've had, get your head under the big blue sky – even if it means poking your head out of the window. The blue spectrums of light I have asked you to avoid in the evening – well, this is their time to shine. Morning light is crucial for triggering the appropriate hormonal response.

REHYDRATE, STRETCH AND BREATHE

After your morning sky-time experience, have a good glug of clean room-temperature water, hit the mat to mobilize your locomotive joints and shake out your face.

- Then hit the 100 cycles of alternate nostril breathing practice from the Breathing and Being chapter (see page 49).

NEXT » OUTDOORS AND INDOORS

- Find the benefits of nature inside and outside.
- Learn how to get skilled in sunlight.
- Invite nature into your home and workspace.

CHAPTER 8

Outdoors and Indoors

As you know, I am all about hunting out and developing simple methods for thriving health that do not cause disruption in one's existing life. To reconnect to the earth, it doesn't get much simpler than freeing your feet and setting off on a shoe-less walk in the grass or on the beach. 'But, Mr Riddle, I live in the city!' I hear you exclaim. And yes, it can be tough to imagine lush forests and woodland when living in a town or city without conjuring up a story of having to travel far, far away to reach them. Panoramic greenery seems like the stuff of fairy tales, right? But it's actually much easier than you think to get your nature fix without leaving your city home. Nature is accessible.

A few years ago I took a group of children to a huge nature park near Windsor. My friends run a creative school for kids in the school holidays and they had asked me to hold a rewilding experience for them. We rocked up at the Savill Garden for a 'Busy Buttons' experience, the children all walking in pairs, ready to walk first around a mix of beautifully manicured areas, then through parts that were just left to grow properly diverse. We went on to a bridge over the lake, then into a meadow. Soon, the kids were all sitting around in a circle, wondering what they could hear if they closed their eyes. You know kids' imaginations! We had 'I can hear a lion' and 'I can hear a tiger'. All very different to adults who tend to come out with 'I'm listening in for a bumblebee or bird'. 'Let's all stand up,' I said. We all stood in a circle and I instructed them to take their shoes and socks off. 'But it's muddy.' I reassured them: 'That's okay. Trust the process.' They took their shoes and socks off. And, as soon as their bare feet hit the ground, it was as if they'd just been let out of a cage. Some had never done this. Can you imagine?! But now they were off the mark, they just ran around like complete lunatics, roaring and screaming.

This was a rewilding. I'd thought kids didn't need rewilding, but this was a clear example that they did. They had not been exposed to the elements and needed that re-childing element. And then my friend who ran the camp said, 'What are we going to do with them now?' And I simply replied, 'We don't do anything. We're just going to stand here and admire what freedom looks like.'

What I still love about that moment is that it reminds me of our adult intellectual mind and how we tend to view 'inappropriate behaviour' for an adult. By watching kids, we really get to see what is beneath it. It's pure emotion. That imagination, the lion and the roaring. When they were given permission, you really got to see what freedom looked like in that moment. 'I've been let out of the cage.' It was beautiful to observe.

Being in nature is not a hit-or-miss experience. Children who grow up with greener surroundings have up to 55% less risk of developing various mental disorders later in life. This is shown by a new study from Aarhus University, Denmark, emphasizing the need to design green and healthy cities for the future.

As a human collective, whether we're consciously aware of

it or not, our senses automatically awaken to the sound of leafy branches crackling in the wind. *It's in our DNA*. As the breeze stirs those branches, it also cleanses us of that city dis-ease, allowing us to think more clearly and regain consciousness.

And when we do get outside and reconnect to the earth with these simple acts, we can immediately feel the warm hug of Mother Nature. It sounds 'woo-woo', I know, but science has my back on this one, too. There's mounting evidence to support what we inherently know deep down in our ancestral bones – that direct contact with the earth's surface may be one of the most beneficial health moves that you can make for yourself. Several studies suggesting myriad health benefits to counteract the plethora of modern diseases can be found by using a simple hashtag: #GETOUTSIDE.

Are you interested in reducing inflammation? Looking for increased cardiovascular health, better immune function, greater sleep quality, faster recovery times? Perhaps you're exploring downregulation of your nervous system to lower stress levels. You might be paying attention to managing your circadian rhythms, trying to regulate cortisol production, serotonin and melatonin. You're surely thinking about the mental health benefits.

> 'Reconnection to the natural world is fundamental to human health, wellbeing, spirit, and survival.'
>
> *Richard Louv*

Taking time out in nature can be seriously underestimated and brushed off by us urbanites. But I personally see time experienced in nature as a potent healing process, in which the effects on our physical, social and spiritual wellbeing are just too profound to be ignored.

By reconnecting to nature immersion through bare skin and breathwork practices, we get to recharge from the battery of life that is Mother Earth. We change our stress-induced, sedentary, linear and grey concrete frequency to reconnect and fall back in love with both our internal and external natural frequency. By removing the insulation of the sensory and insulated rubber-soled shoe, we connect to the biodiversity underfoot – from the rich forest floors to the wildflowers of meadows; from the soft sands of our coastlines to the rocky trail of our mountains. We receive the healing vibes from the earth's potent anti-inflammatory superpowers.

The more biodiverse, the more potent the emotional experiences, the higher I've lifted my vibe. Getting high, not just on my own supply, but from the mother of all suppliers. If you're looking for something similar yourself, this doesn't mean you have to go full butt-naked. To reconnect to what humans were once at one with, you simply have to expose your bare feet, get grounded under your favourite tree, open up your field of vision and inhale that environment. Just 20 minutes in a forest is proven to radically reduce stress hormones like cortisol and adrenaline.

Even a short amount of time outside is enough to have a positive impact on reducing symptoms of stress. Then, taking it a little further, if we find a green space, remove our shoes and open up all our senses, we give ourselves up to nature's potent healing powers. We start to recognize that this is more than symptom relief, that nature connects us to understanding the cause. And the more time we can connect to this profound teaching that the natural world provides, the more we can identify with what we need to do to thrive – not just in the forest, but when we re-enter the indoor environment, be it the home or the workspace.

A larger and larger share of the world's population now lives in cities and the World Health Organization estimates that more than 450 million of the global human population suffer from a mental disorder, a number that is expected to increase. If you have a full-on job, or like me you're juggling family life and work, getting your 10% supplementation of forest bathing isn't always an option. For some, it might not be possible to get to a green space every day. But that doesn't mean we can't invite nature in.

My own nature-immersive time in the forest led me to wondering about how we could invite the forest in. What if we could create an office-based or home forest bathing experience? More and more studies are proving that inviting nature into both the home and workspace, through interior plant walls (living, not plastic!) and indoor trees, can have a profound effect on reducing stress, enhancing creativity and helping us achieve flow states – just like those 20-minute hits of GETOUTSIDE time.

Mother Nature's medicine cabinet

Researchers from the University of Exeter's Medical School recently analysed mental health data from 10,000 city dwellers. Using high-resolution mapping to track where subjects had lived over an 18-year period, they found that people living near more green space were reported to have up to 55% lower risk of developing a mental disorder. This was even after adjusting for income, education and employment (all of which are also correlated with health).

In 2009, a team of Dutch researchers found a lower incidence of 15 diseases – including depression, anxiety, heart disease, diabetes, asthma and migraines – in people who lived within about a half mile of green space. And, in 2015, an international team overlaid health questionnaire responses from more than 31,000 Toronto residents on to a map of the city, block by block. Those living in blocks with more trees showed a boost in heart and metabolic health equivalent to what one would experience from a $20,000 gain in income. Lower mortality and fewer stress hormones circulating in the blood have also been connected to living close to green space.

There is, of course, so much more at play than just grounding and tuning into our natural frequency. When we step out of the concrete jungle and return to the forests, woods or meadows – basking under the canopies of the trees or bathing in the healing sunlight among the plants – we get hit by an abundance of a release of compounds called terpenes. When we inhale, these aromatic terpenes increase the body's natural killer cells and help support our immune system.

True terpenes and pioneer cannabis researcher Dr Ethan Russo found that terpenes 'could produce synergy with respect to treatment of pain, inflammation, depression, anxiety, addiction, epilepsy, cancer, fungal and bacterial infections'. The essential oils revolution has brought with it scientific research and awareness of the medical benefits of terpenes and aromatherapy.

When we return our skin back to the soil we experience the diversity of that soil. Microbial soils give us a symbiotic experience, while the grey concrete city gives us one of dysbiosis. Which one do you want your skin to be inhaling? Now can you see why diversity is key: diversity in the soil, diversity in the plants, diversity for the plethora of benefits inhaled by the human experience enabling us to be more biodiverse, as beings of planet Earth.

In a mind-blowing study, researchers in Finland recreated the environmental biodiversity of a forest floor on the playgrounds of four urban daycare centres by covering the playgrounds with forest soil, moss, meadow grasses, dwarf heather, blueberries and crowberries and installed planter boxes for growing garden crops. The children were encouraged to play and interact with their newly created forest floor for 90 minutes a day for 28 days. The scientists then analysed changes in the skin and gut microbiota and blood immune markers during the 28-day biodiversity intervention.

The gut and skin microbes of all the children were analysed before and after the experiment and were compared with children from other urban daycare centres with standard urbanized playyards – it doesn't take much to visualize linear concrete and tarmac with painted lines.

What came out of the study was really quite profound. After just one month of connecting to the biodiversity of the manipulated playground forest floor, the diversity of the children's skin and intestinal bacteria increased quite dramatically, as did their T-cells and other important immune markers in their blood work. 'We also found that the intestinal microbiota of children [who were playing in this nursery greenery] was similar to the intestinal microbiota of children visiting the forest every day,' explained environmental scientist Marja Roslund from the University of Helsinki in 2020. 'This supports the assumption that contact with nature prevents disorders in the immune system, such as autoimmune diseases and allergies,' research scientist Aki Sinkkonen concluded, and 'low biodiversity in the modern living environment may lead to an uneducated immune system and consequently increase the prevalence of immune-mediated diseases'.

Grounding practice

We are a small intimate group, working with Pablo, a shaman. Pablo has 12 stations set around a lake. Each of us is going to be dropped off at one of these locations, out of sight of one another. Every hour, Pablo will come and walk each individual around to the next station. The practice is called a solar rotation. Twelve hours on, we will all reconnect and share our profound insights by the fire. The idea is to listen to the guidance of an 'uncle' and make notes. On days like these, I can fill a whole notebook. The messages are simple, profound, yet with a real sense of an uncle's familiarity. Today, Ian, an incredible artist from the tribe, has brought some bubble wrap for us all to sit on, a really thoughtful and nice thing to do, right? But the uncle doesn't see it this way. My first lesson is how incredibly disconnected we are. After all, we are here around the lake to reconnect to nature, to lift the veil and tune in to nature's profound wisdom. And yet here we are with bubble wrap to protect us from the earth. Wanting very much to get plugged in, only to become even more unplugged from the supercharge of life's battery, just through the insulating bubble wrap. In my journal, I write 'No More Bubble Wrap'. No more disconnection from nature and her healing capacity. But this only confirms and reinforces my desire to walk barefoot. So, off come my shoes. Once again, I move barefoot over the earth, grounding.

Grounding refers to the reconnection of our body into the earth. When we move barefoot over terrain, the skin of our feet creates an electrical conduit to the blanket of electrons that flow above the soil. It is, of course, not just our feet that get hit with the supercharge of nature: our whole bodies are plugged in.

We are children of the sun

It's fundamental for us equatorial apes that we take a hit of the big blue in the morning before it hits afternoon light. A sunny morning will provide a shot of anywhere between 20,000 and 100,000 units of light (known as lux) to your ancestral eyes. Bright natural light in the morning dumps out melatonin, which immediately makes you feel more alert without having to smash the caffeine. Exposure to that bright early morning light also helps the healthy release of cortisol and our happy hormone serotonin – which is also necessary for the synthesis of melatonin. Let's say the average light bulb is 60 to 1000 lux. I'll take sunny sky time over screen time any day of the week.

SEROTONIN: NATURE'S ANTIDEPRESSANT

Serotonin is a getting-high-on-our-own-supply hormone that is associated with happiness and boosting mood. The early light aligns our central circadian clock in the brain, acting like a reset button. This cue triggers the rest of the body into syncing regulatory systems – your digestion, hormones, immune system, neurotransmitters, etc. Without this signal, you would be more prone to a circadian hormonal cascade, which can cause the common modern-day malaise. Bright natural light in the morning helps you feel more alert, providing an optimal amount of cortisol, increasing body temperature: improved mood and better focus, more suitable to good work performance. In the evening, lower light cues the body the other way. More melatonin and less serotonin is needed for falling asleep and getting deeper sleep.

Having ginger hair, pasty skin and freckles as a child meant I was given a one-way ticket to sun-worshipping Worrierville. Aside from all the name-calling associated with the above, I was always educated in the great fearful topic of sun avoidance. As I would burn like a vampire the moment the sun appeared, I should apply the highest factors of suncream on my porcelain-white bod. As a result, going on holiday would mean walking around like an oiled-up Channel swimmer.

I've had many 'stay out of the sun' moments and debates with my trusted tribal elders on the subject of sun exposure. How could I argue back? SPF ad campaigns and the heavily chemical-laden suncream manufacturers had nailed that one. When skin cancer hit the news, my chances of ever tanning were gone in a moment. My parents never questioned it.

I started to hate the summer months, dreading the sun. Due to my inflammatory diet, I was known as 'allergy boy'. I had the most horrendous case of hay fever known to humanity, which meant that for those few months of the year I was immobilized by fear, eyes red raw, skin sunburnt and sneezing uncontrollably. It wasn't hard for anyone to understand why summer just wasn't my thing.

Most people choose to chase the sun but I'd become so fearful of it, I would be suncreamed up to the eyeballs, covered up sitting in the shade. Many years of sun avoidance went by, without questioning why. After all, the social tribe would know, right? My trusted tribal elders: parents, doctor, pharmacist, supermarkets, the press – they couldn't all be wrong, could they?

Well, as it turns out, the boy who feared the sun has had a complete shift of habit. Yes, I threw away the suncream and developed a base tan. The same guy known as allergy boy – who no longer has allergies, no longer looks like burnt boy – now loves the sun and can be found sun-gazing at any appropriate moment. And it is all about the appropriate moment.

I wasn't alone in fearing the sun. Yet the sun *is* nature, we need it in our normal human biology. Before the suncream industry sprang up in the middle of the last century, the sun – and sunlight – was recognized as a potent healer.

SUNLIGHT THERAPY

Between the late 19th to the mid-20th century, heliotherapy, AKA sunlight therapy, was considered to be the most efficacious treatment for diseases. Exposing patients to controlled amounts of sunlight was found to dramatically lower elevated blood pressure, cholesterol counts and blood sugar in diabetics, as well as increase the number of white blood cells. By 1933, sunlight was proving to be a beneficial treatment for many diseases, including gout, TB, rheumatoid arthritis, colitis, arteriosclerosis, anaemia, cystitis, eczema, acne, psoriasis, herpes, lupus, sciatica, kidney problems, asthma and even burns.

What surprised the pioneers of heliotherapy the most was the fact that the sun's potent healing rays were less effective if the patients wore sunglasses. Sunglasses block out important rays of the light spectrum picked up from the eye and around the eye, which the body requires for essential biological functions.

Dr Auguste Rollier, the father of heliotherapy, found that sunbathing early in the morning, in conjunction with a nutritious diet, provided the most effective benefits.

The sun has huge healing powers that require a set of skills in us to harness its full effects; in this way sunlight is NO different to movement, food, digestion, sleep. All we need is the right input to gain the crucial 'how to' messages to eternal growth. Sunlight boosts serotonin, the happy hormone, and enables us to synthesize vitamin D3. Honestly, do we think that getting bathed in artificial lights and sprayed with chemicals is going to be better for us than healing in the sun?

RED OR OFF TO BED

Infrared light is a spectrum of light that we can't see, but which has a profound healing effect on our wellbeing and plays a crucial role in leading a 'heal-thy' lifestyle. You sense infrared light as 'heat'. The heat you feel from the sun or from the glow of the fire – that's those infrared feels. Infrared has an effect on cell health by expanding water that's responsible for pushing toxins out of our cells. Infrared and near infrared also strengthen the mitochondria – the powerhouse of the cell and where the cell's energy is created. You could go all out and start gathering in the great outdoors under the big blue sky and, once it gets dark, light a fire to huddle up around. Hugging is also something else to consider. The heat from another person's skin, that's infrared, too.

XPA is protein that has been found to play a part in healing the damage caused by UV radiation. XPA protein activity is significantly higher in the morning than in the evening. By aligning with our circadian rhythm, the XPA protein can fix errors in our DNA caused by UV radiation. When XPA is low, these errors go unrepaired, heightening the risk of cancer.

Tommy, an old client of mine, had been fortunate enough to catch a mole that a biopsy had shown as skin cancer. Quite the reserved English gent, Tommy was a little confused, as he couldn't recall ever showing his peachy white bottom to the sun, yet here he was with skin cancer. We are now spending less and less time outdoors. When we are outdoors, we slather our skin in synthetic chemical SPFs. And we still get skin cancer?

New treatments using light are increasingly being recognized as breakthrough methods for cancer and many other diseases. Although it has been known for over 100 years that light can kill diseased cells, it's taken a number of convincing research studies to produce a recent resurgence of interest in light therapy. Regular, short exposure to sunlight, at the right time of day – without burning – still seems to be one of the most beneficial measures one can take to prevent many diseases, including some cancers of the skin.

Yes, it is a skill to harness the healing benefits of sun exposure. When exposing your skin, there's the time of day to consider, along with the hormones that we hold to repair the damage of the sun. We have to be mindful when travelling. If you live in England and decide to move to Northern Australia, you'll increase your exposure by 600%! Calculations show that for every six miles you move closer to the equator, you increase your exposure to UV light by 1%. So, remember the sun is not equal everywhere. You have to acclimatize your skin and build your own defensive mechanism.

- Remember, UV radiation is lower in the morning, as the sun is sitting lower in the sky.

- Hit yourself up with 1 hour per day of sunlight if you want to build your base tan, keep your cholesterol in check, lower your blood pressure and blood sugar and increase white blood cells.
- Even if it's cloudy or raining, get out into nature as often as possible. Expose as much skin as you can before 11am.
- In the afternoons, wear appropriate clothing to shield yourself. Avoid chemical suncreams and always choose organic over inorganic.
- Remember that it's not necessary to always wear sunglasses when you're outdoors.

Introducing the outdoors to the indoors

We can't all live in nature, but that doesn't mean we can't live naturally. There are multiple reasons as to why we humans enjoy the outdoors and natural light, and they mostly stem from an inner desire to reconnect with nature. And if we know this to be true in our outdoor environments, then it seems that a really simple solution would be to invite nature into our everyday habitats.

We want to thrive, we want to flourish, we want to be at the top of our game, we want to be killing it, but the habitats that we are spending the most time in could in actual fact be killing us. The concentrations of toxins in our indoor spaces are often 2–5 times more potent than those outdoors – particularly in those enclosed rooms where we sleep over an accumulative amount of time.

Wherever humans are we also find rats, so let me now turn to Bruce K. Alexander and his Rat Park Studies in the late 1970s, at Simon Fraser University, Vancouver, Canada. Discovering

Alexander's study was like acknowledging that we are existing in a Human Laboratory. The aim of his experiment was to prove that, rather than drugs causing addiction, it's actually down to the living environment. Alexander wanted to disprove existing studies that connected opiate addiction in laboratory rats to addictive properties within the drug itself.

Constructing a rat park with toys for play, free access to food and mating space, Alexander introduced 16–20 rats of each sex to the park. He tested a variety of theories, using different experiments within the rat park against a group of rats kept in solitary confinement without the same space and facility to play, mate and eat at will. The social rats had the choice to drink fluids from one of two dispensers; one contained plain tap water, the other a morphine solution.

He then ran experiments to test the park rats' willingness to consume the morphine solution compared with the rats kept in solitary confinement. They found that the caged rats ingested around 19 times more morphine solution than park rats. The park rats consistently resisted the morphine water, preferring to opt for the plain water.

More astounding still, the caged rats that were fed nothing but morphine water for 57 days chose plain water when they were moved to the rat park, voluntarily going through withdrawal from the morphine.

No matter what they tried, Alexander and his team produced nothing that resembled addiction in rats that were housed in the rat park.

Based on the study, Alexander concluded that drugs themselves do not cause addictions – rather, a person's environment feeds an addiction. Feelings of isolation, loneliness, hopelessness and lack of control based on unsatisfactory living conditions make a person dependent on substances.

Under biologically normal living conditions, resistance to drugs and alcohol is natural – as the study demonstrated, addiction is a pacifier to a lack. It's a logical conclusion, then, that living in an environment which supports our needs and does not create any illusion of lack (as the modern urban environment can) will eradicate addiction as an emotional support. Like the rats of the rat park, we urbanites have been removed from our natural habitat and dropped into disinfected, linear, circadian rhythm-disrupting, overstimulating, chronically stressful, concrete, sedentary-promoting, toxic settings – human cages, if you will.

So, how do we flip it? How do we transform our home and work environments into giant grow bags?

Think of the bedroom where you breathe the same air in and out for up to eight hours each night, between the same four walls. It's where you spend a third of your life. When asking people I coach how many years they have been inhaling the same bedroom experience, their answer has been years and years (and years). And they respond from the point of view of continuity and stability and security – all those things. For one person, it was 50 years in the same bedroom. The very few things that might have changed for their experience were the colours on the walls or their mattress. When I dropped in the neurotoxin conversation around paints, mastics, glues and soft furnishing versus indigenous bedrooms of natural materials exposed to clean air, you should have seen the expression of discomfort on their faces!

So if you're going into the same bedroom box in the same four-walled house, then into the same kitchen box to experience exactly the same breakfast, not sensing foods that smell exactly the same, what new experience are you getting, what new neurological or physical wiring or rewiring? Your microbiome is deadening. You are not uploading any new information to what should be a forever growing, forever rewiring, nourished species. And that's the overlooked and disconnected truth that needs to be faced by the modern urbanite species.

Make ancestral magic work for you

Just like our ancestors and modern-day hunter-gatherers, we could reconnect our urbanite selves with the plants, rocks, trees and animals and be part of the landscape. We could become the very ecosystem in which we live. What if we viewed our shelter as an opportunity to tick multiple fundamental need boxes? Instead of it being in the Human Laboratory, we flip the Human Park switch, so that each day another satisfied, happy human pops out?

What if we created home and work spaces that we actually wanted to keep returning to, because we feel a profound sense of wellbeing each and every time we revisit?

Dr Stuart Brown (see page 90) is quoted as saying the opposite of play is not work; it's depression. But if your environment isn't one that ticks the growth-promoting box, then play in this environment isn't quite going to work for you. If you want to improve performance, concentration, creativity, boost energy and maintain a healthful and vibrant existence, the primary habitat that informs these habits needs to shift accordingly.

It's quite baffling that we sensorial, cellular, microbial beings have normalized spending a whopping 90% of our day inside sterile linear boxes. But for those that have been conditioned into thinking that this is the norm, then the solution is to cast your rewilding lens over the habitat in which you spend the most of your time. If it's not practical in this moment in time to get outside, you have to invite nature in.

> Clutter can play a significant role in how we feel about our homes, our workplaces, and ourselves. Messy homes and workspaces leave us feeling anxious, helpless, and overwhelmed. Yet, rarely is clutter recognized as a significant source of stress in our lives.
>
> *Psychology Today*

Clean up the air, remove the toxic materials, bring more nature in. Every time you breathe in and out, every time you touch something natural, you get a microbiotic experience. And the great point here is that you don't have to keep having the same experience. Just like the ever-changing natural landscape 'out there', you can change it up 'in here' and get that rewiring sensory experience. Can you imagine it?

We have to accept that, yeah, we are living indoors, we are this new urbanite species, AKA the indoor generation, but there it is, we can flip it. Start by ensuring that we at least get that 10% of our time outdoors and honouring that commitment. We *can* go outside, experience nature and get to the green spaces. Even if you don't have a garden, this is easier than you might think.

Take London, for instance. There are 3,000 parks and 30,000 allotments, where you can get your hands in the dirt and inhale the earth and feed that microbiome. There are over 8.4 million trees in London. That's nearly one tree for each of 8.6 million Londoners to explore, hug, climb, explore, or even sit beneath and meditate or look at in awe. London has been awarded the title as the largest urban forest; meaning it is almost the perfect environment for the modern urbanite to go 10% wild in. It drops London into the same realms as Sherwood Forest near Nottingham or the New Forest in Hampshire.

When we start to gain more understanding of what our natural frequency is, we can start looking for how we can bring more nature *inside* – how we can invite nature into our indoor environment to help us maintain it.

Steps to rewilding outdoors and indoors

When we reconnect to the biodiversity of nature underfoot and raise our vibration through breathwork, we radically shift our state of being. It's the triple whammy of **nature immersion, skin-to-earth contact** and **down-regulation breath** that enables that deep level of connection to something much bigger than ourselves.

GET SKY TIME OVER SCREEN TIME

How much time are you spending *outside*? I don't mean in the shops, in the car or on public transport. These are all *indoors*. How many hours are you under the blue, white and grey, serotonin-enhancing sky? How much time are you spending under the sky, without looking down at your screen? In the UK, 83% of us live in urban environments, spending on average 90% of our life indoors.

- This practice is super-simple. Leave your phone at home or at the office. Set a timer and try to accumulate your 10% sky-in-the-ancestral-eye time, every day.
- Do it again and again. Remember, this is an accumulation, so it can be achieved incrementally.

UPGRADE YOUR SENSES

Get into the habit of asking yourself how many senses you're receiving. And how organic is this information you're choosing to upgrade your senses with? My recommendation with this practice is to rewild your senses by actively going in search of more natural experiences. I'm not just talking nose, eyes, ears here. The more spiritual skin in the game, the more heightened the experience. Think sensory genomics, rewiring your mind–body loop.

- It doesn't get much simpler than freeing your feet and setting off on a mindful shoeless walk.
- Be mindful of what you're experiencing when you return your skin back to the soil. You're inhaling the diversity in that microbial soil through your skin, gaining a symbiotic experience.
- Create a wider visual field to fully scope your environment. Our hyper-visual screen-time eyes stimulate a sympathetic response, whereas our panoramic visual field stimulates a parasympathetic one.

SEEK OUT BIODIVERSITY

The more diverse the natural experience, the more heightened the emotional experience. This practice is about taking that sky-time over screen-time practice and actively seeking out nature's abundance.

- Become intimate with nature. Sit, breathe, relax into it, perhaps using the self-intimacy practice from the Breathing and Being chapter (see page 68).
- Write a journal about your nature experiences. How did it feel to connect your feet to the soils, sands, grasses, mossy forest floors? How different were the experiences when immersing in the cold waters of the seas, lakes, rivers, ponds? How does it feel to walk and inhale the plant-based medicines of the forests or ancient woodlands vs the flowery meadows? What wildlife did you see, out with life that is wild?

GROW A FUTURE

Our wild habit no doubt nourishes our wellbeing, but how well is nature itself? We need to make steps to growing a wilder future. You can join the environmental rewilding movement by taking small steps to grow and protect our biodiversity.

- Sign up to a reforesting programme, getting involved in tree-planting ceremonies, gifting friends and loved ones a tree or a number of planted trees.
- Get behind organizations that are defending the defenders of our extraordinary biodiversity – that's the indigenous communities who protect 80% of our global biodiversity, while constantly having to fight for their lands and their rights.

- Visit and support rewilding and regenerative projects, estates and farms.

GRAB SOME SUNLIGHT

When the early sun is sitting low on the horizon it offers very little to no UV radiation, but still offers all the amazing healing benefits. Early sun hits us with potent infrared and also helps regulate our hormones: out with the hormones associated with sleep and in with the hormones associated with your daytime wake time.

- Get up and out to receive the healing morning sun.
- Expose your eyes and as much spiritual skin as your socially norm templates will allow you to.

CREATE YOUR RITUALISTIC SPACE

My own nature-immersive time has helped me understand what parts of nature I would like to invite in. Now it's your turn to gather the intel to create your very own home- or office-based forest bathing experience. Find a space that you're energetically drawn to in your home and make it your 'go-to' space for being with yourself.

- Use this space for your ritualistic self-care practice. Fill it with plants.
- Check the Breathing and Being chapter for ways to sit with yourself and ways to breathe in the space.

LIVE AT GROUND LEVEL

You've read my advice about decluttering and minimalizing indoors. You may already be casting your ancestral eye over your indoor habitat, wondering how you can make the shift to more natural materials, views, scents and living organic materials. If there's a chair there, you'll want to sit on it. This is about creating a space or spaces that will honour your natural sitting practice. Think ceremonial, ritualistic spaces, where no chairs exist. This can be for dining, working, Netflix bingeing, reading, breathwork, meditation, even reading the morning paper – whatever ritual you want to adopt.

- Low-sitting furniture – tables, desks or low cushions – help to create something more desirable than parking your paleo butt in a chair. Low-sitting dining tables with beautiful cushions will transform your dining experience.
- Perhaps commit to eating one of your meals 'ground-living style', or answering your emails while getting your squat on.

BREATHE BETTER WITH PLANTS

We want the air in our home and workspace to be growth-promoting, not compromising. Plants can help, as long as you're mindful that they lose 50% of their purifying potency for every metre they're away from natural light.

- Do a bit of research about indoor plants and bring them into your indoor life. They'll stimulate your senses and feed your soul.
- Consider an air purifier – it'll do what it says, removing 99.97% of allergens, pollutants and gases.

GET INTO LIGHT

Although I've covered the importance of light elsewhere, I can't emphasize enough how crucial it is to make the shift to creating the appropriate circadian lighting experience.

- Wake yourself up in the morning by getting outside under the early sky – even when cloudy.
- Create biological darkness in the evenings when the sun has gone down. This doesn't mean a blackout, just establishing the same light tones as if you had fire, stars and moon.
- Seek out sunlight and firelight for those mitochondria gains. Try rewilding yourself with those fireside chats, sweat lodges or perhaps find an infrared sauna or bring some red light tech therapy into your indoor experience.

NEXT » BEING MORE HUMAN

- By now you're already being more human and embracing interdependence.
- Find your community, set your intention and overcome fear of abandonment.
- Discover some useful resources for your ongoing journey.

Conclusion: Being More Human

By this point, depending on how you've been using the book, you'll probably have tried out a few exercises from Part Two. You might be wondering just how long it's going to take you to 'be more human'. Let me tell you right here that you're on the journey just by having got this far. You are already 'being more human'.

There's a lot we can learn from indigenous communities. They understand the natural world and are expert conservationists. They often put the community before the individual, sharing and exchanging possessions rather than amassing personal wealth, and embrace gender equality. I hope you realize by now that I'm not suggesting that you embrace the Hadza way of life in the city. Instead, I'm asking us all to work towards reconnecting to communities with ways of living that are better for the human and the environment, communities that help honour collective health and wellbeing.

In this final chapter I want to help you on your way by giving you pointers to lots of places and people to look up and go to – some I've mentioned in the book. I trust you'll get something out of the resources section that makes up most of this chapter (see page 214).

Finding community, setting intention

Let me finish my invitation to Be More Human by welcoming you into my 100 Human Experience.

The 100 Human Experience started out as a workshop we called Move Breathe Chill, which I delivered with my breathwork brother, Artur Paulins. These workshops were a potent combination of playful movement, breathwork and ice baths. In their infancy they were quite intimate, with groups of just 16–20 people, but I really wanted more people to feel the potency of this work. So my goal became to make this experience much more accessible by holding space for many more humans to come together. The 100 Human Experience was born.

Up until that point I'd held the 100 Human Experience in London, which meant indoors. Yet my whole philosophy is about making a deeper connection to nature, be it through inner work and finding inner understanding that we are nature, or reconnecting and immersing in the great outdoor sense of nature. And so the obvious path to hold the hand of 100 humans would be to take the 100 Human Experience out into nature.

It was amazing to see stiff physical and social structures being dismantled and deconstructed through re-childing play and rewilding human movements. On a misty Saturday morning, I saw people dropping layers – of clothing and conditioning. Witnessing the profundity of the playful state of mind can be quite something for the observer. You could literally see the shedding of the physical facade – the armoury falling away, as 100 strangers warmed to one another and moulded under a collective force field where time had no real meaning. The wet dewy grass became the perfect environment for feet to feel wild again and the senses to reawaken. We had created a space where wrestling, hugging, being held and rolling around in the dewy grass in the morning mist were now socially normal. We placed our foreheads together and took it in turns to mirror the other's movements. We became the annoying drunken friend who keeps falling over and becoming a nuisance, while our sober partners have to play a supportive role and stop us from falling to the ground. I'd asked the warmed-up and open beautiful beings of Planet Earth to form a huge circle, now standing shoulder to shoulder, barefoot and grounded, open and empowered. I then guided them to make their way to the centre of the circle and back out to the other side, to reform the circle of power. If they made eye contact with anyone while navigating the path to reforming the circle, they would then stop, hold their fellow humans by the shoulder and roar with intention the words 'You are loved' into each other's eyes, then hug and move again. We would repeat and repeat until the words felt authentic and complete. This was in the post-Covid lockdown era of 2021 and, after months of being socially distanced from fellow beings, the emotional release and reconnection to the physical need of human contact felt so raw, so potent and – well – so needed. It was in this moment, with goosebumps and the hairs standing on the back of my neck, that I said to Artur, 'I f**king love holding space.'

The breathwork session flowed beautifully, unscrewing the intellectual lid and diving deep down into belly-raw emotions and back up and out to the universe. The play experience opened the perfect portal to the stripping away of layers of resistance. Artur felt it, we all felt it – there's something really powerful about holding breathwork sessions in nature. The elements of course played their role – the sounds, the scents, the sun breaking through the misty morning air, the gentle breeze. But then, with the layers dropped, we were a community feeling every bit a part of those elements, this collective sense of being connected.

The fire pit also became a communal experience where people were playing African drums in preparation to immerse in their own rite of passage in the ice bath, all while maintaining their tuned-in state. Then, back to reforming a circle. Suddenly, in stepped the beautiful shining light that is Kate Lister, a voice-awakening coach. She was with us to hold space with her ukulele around the fire, all for the rewilding of voice – where the collective chanting, shouting, singing, Omming and belly laughter helped each and every one of us reconnect to our voice, releasing all that has gone unsaid, deconstructing and dismantling all those years of being told to be quiet and sit still. All of the censored and unspoken truths could be let out, healing the throat chakras of many, and all flowing seamlessly around the fire that kept burning and warming everyone throughout the night.

After communal cooking, where my NatLife tribe members contributed to the weekend experience by bringing food, we spent the night at the fire, setting intention to wake in the morning, with the fire still burning. I shared how I felt that this 100 Human Experience would provide such hope. The feelings of love, connection, joy and being held as one interdependent force were undeniably strong. Those feelings emphasized even more how important it is for us, as innately wild, connected and empowered beings, to immerse in healthy and natural lifestyle communities. And to embrace experiences that help shake and awaken us from the normalized, disempowering social attachments and behaviours that have inhibited us from reaching our individual and collective potential. How it really matters to take part in lifestyle-changing practices in the company of like-minded people who want to improve their health, wellbeing and refine their human experience. I ended by asking everyone to imagine what could be achieved if we were all motivated by love, connection and joy.

Words will never do the experience of that weekend justice – especially the huge collective primal roar of 'I am grateful' around the giant ice bath.

Overcoming our fear of abandonment

Why is it so tough to honour the decision to step outside the social attachments and behaviours that have inhibited Homo sapiens from reaching our individual and collective potential?

Perhaps the answer lies in the vast vaults of our evolution as social primates. In the early evolution of our humankind, when we were living in small groups, our ability to form alliances and collaborate enabled us to survive and later thrive. Those that collaborated communicated best, perhaps even conformed; they survived. Whereas those that didn't conform, or meet the requirements of the collective, could face being ostracized. In a world of large predators, this would most likely not have ended well for the abandoned individual.

Is it that this fear of abandonment resides so deep in our primordial mind that we will make decisions of conformity at the slightest hint of our place within the social group being threatened? If we can park that fear of abandonment, we soon recognize that we're never alone. I hope I've shown you throughout this book that we can step outside what can become limiting, toxic or unnatural social norms that we no longer feel resonate with our beliefs. Instead, we consciously drop into new communities, aligned to and supporting our values.

If we can put that fear aside, we can see that, no matter what the social norm, it is always best to reconnect with our natural norms. This book began by describing the day I finally realized that for years I'd been spending my money on all the wrong stuff, pacifying my suffering, pleasure-seeking through objects of distraction. This was the day I started to thrive. All of my little uploads – from shopping, scrolling, eating out, drinking and drugs – were all just socially normalized moments of hedonistic escape, none of which ever delivered their promised happiness. Once I realized that it was an inside job, I quit the pleasure-seeking, limiting behaviours and found my freedom in a community of like-minded individuals, who helped steer each other's focus towards what we actually needed to thrive. I learned that to be successful was to be content. We also learned to spend our money on things which genuinely satisfied our biologically normal needs and that were good for the human and good for the environment.

If you follow me on social media, you may be wondering how we socially integrate our kids, given that they are unschooled (or home-schooled). Well, we use the great platform of social media for its amazing benefits (you see, screens aren't all bad when it's about connection). We look for unschooling and home-schooling groups in the area. We want to immerse ourselves in a community that has like-minded people who are looking to live a natural lifestyle that's good for the human and good for the environment. If we have the right intentions with social media, we can use it for social change.

When we lived in Ibiza, we picked up some incredible experiences, from fire ceremonies to drumming circles and crystal healing, by seeing things outside of our social templates and inherited behaviours. By putting aside our fear of abandonment, we've always been able to slot into something new. When we wanted to move out of London, down to Cornwall or Somerset, we couldn't find anything. I knew that something would come up, because it always does. And serendipity stepped in, with my friend Seth and his beautiful 42 Acres retreat venue in Somerset, where there was accommodation waiting to be filled.

So we dropped into 42 Acres with Seth and his partner Renata. Katerina and the kids just loved it. There was a whole community of families, on this amazing biodynamic, regenerative farm. The kids got to hang out with other kids, living in a close-knit community at a time when everything was closed up in the UK, people were in lockdown. One location, enough on the land to live off the land. This was a real opportunity to see how you could really live it and be it. And now, this is very much how I see community.

After six months, we needed to find another place. I found a house west of 42 Acres, near Frome. As the house was rural, we started to look into forging links, looking for unschooling/home-schooling groups in the area, dropping into different events – but just not feeling it. My thought was that we should hold out for the community we feel we're aligned with. We were removing that fear of abandonment, accepting that there was so much out there. There was no need to worry about being alone. One day I was out for a run, when someone saw me and direct-messaged me to say there's 100 of us in this area and we're totally aligned. Been following you, love your work, there's a number of us that meet up here. What that told me was that even if you can't find the community, you can always build something and people will come, because others are out there searching as well.

We are now involved in setting up a forest school with another couple of families, and someone has donated their land to the project. So, we can have a space for the kids, with a yurt, a fire and woodland. They can have this amazing experience and get their social integration while the parents meet. Yes, the community over there didn't work for us, but don't fill the space up if it's not working, leave the space available, leave it open. Don't be governed by the fear of being on your own. If you set the intention, you'll find it. That really worked for us. And it can for you, too.

'The world is a community of organisms – these organisms, in the mass, determine the environmental influence on any one of them . . . Thus, the community as an environment is responsible for the survival of the separate individuals which compose it, and these separate individuals are responsible for their contributions to the environment.'

A.N. Whitehead

Resources

To help you fully immerse in the realm of interdependence and community, here are some resources from me and from those that have inspired me to be more human. I trust they will be able to hold your hand along the path to rewilding your life and finding what it is to be more human.

NatLife

NatLife Tribe
The NatLife Tribe is a growing health and natural lifestyle community where we take part in real lifestyle conversations, natural movement and breathwork classes, all in the company of like-minded people who also wish to improve their health, wellbeing and refine their human experience.
www.tonyriddle.com/nat-life-tribe-home

NatLife Balance Beams
Reconnecting with a daily balancing practice is not only playful and fun, it is a powerful practice for rewilding the functions of our feet, ankles, knees and hips, which are ultimately the foundations of the beautiful upright posture nature intended you to have.
www.tonyriddle.com/shop/15-balance-beam

NatLife Coach

Join a growing community of Natural Lifestyle Coaches to help others reboot their inner nature, rewild their lives and reconnect to ways of living that are better for the human and better for the environment.

www.tonyriddle.com

Move • Breathe • Chill

This 100 Human Experience is an opportunity to get involved in a growing health and natural lifestyle community. To take part in lifestyle-changing practices, all in the company of like-minded people who also wish to reach their human and our collective potential.

www.tonyriddle.com/move-breathe-chill

Retreats

Rewilding Human Experience

Provides the space and tools for you to reconnect with what your eco human needs, NOT what your human ego wants. To make significant change happen, immerse fully in the healing and trans-formative process of nature, away from everyday life. Let go of the old compromised self – and all that isn't serving you. Explore new ground and emerge with new skills, habits and perspectives to build mental fortitude. Welcome in the wild, connected and empowered version of you.

This four-day experience is filled with an abundance of rewilding: nature immersion natural movements, mobility, wild swimming, human contact, connection and communication, barefoot walks, wild running and down-in-the-dirt playful bear-crawling fun. We tune in and tune up with lots of nourishing rest, sleep, guided meditations, fire ceremonies, drumming and breathwork. We feed our super-natural souls with super-natural foods and lots of belly laughter. **www.tonyriddle.com/retreats**

Rewilding Human Movement

In this 10-day course I'll show you how to build healthy variability into your movement routine and create greater resilience in your physical body. You'll discover and learn:

- How to break out of our modern 'Human Zoo' and rediscover your body's natural movement patterns
- How to reduce and prevent chronic pain
- How to sit, stand, run, jump and hang more efficiently
- Ways to improve your balance, posture and joint mobility
- Techniques for rebooting your mood through movement
- How to enjoy exercise again.

By practising these techniques, you will enjoy more mobility, less chronic pain and an ease of movement that makes exercise playfully joyful once again.
www.onecommune.com/
rewilding-human-movement-free-5-day-pass-sign-up

Podcasts and tutorials

The Natural Lifestylist Podcast
www.tonyriddle.com/podcasts

The Natural Life-Stylist Rewilding Tutorials
Fast-track your rewilding movement journey with Tony's three video tutorials: Rewild Your Squat, Natural Running and Chair Sitting Offsetting.
www.tonyriddle.com/rewilding-tutorials

Breathwork inspiration

Dan Brule
Dan is a modern-day teacher, healer and a world-renowned pioneer in the field of breathwork. He is one of the creators of Breath Therapy, and was among the original group of Internationally Certified Rebirthers. He is a master of Prana Yoga (the Hindu Science of Breath) and Chi Kung/Qigong (Chinese Medical Breathing Exercises), and he leads the worldwide Spiritual Breathing Movement.
https://breathmastery.com/

Patrick McKeown
The Oxygen Advantage Programme is based on Patrick McKeown's experience of working with thousands of clients and hundreds of healthcare professionals, along with his extensive research on breath-hold training over the past 15 years.
https://oxygenadvantage.co.uk/

Artur Paulins

Creator of Breathwork Academy and the explorer of human equanimity, Artur Paulins is working internationally to transform our access to daily calm through coaching and breathwork.
https://www.arturpaulins.com/

Movement inspiration

Katy Bowman

'I propose that movement, like food, is not optional; that ailments you may be experiencing are simply (and complexly) symptoms of movement hunger in response to a movement diet that is dangerously low in terms of quantity and poor in terms of quality – meaning you aren't getting the full spectrum of movement nutrition necessary for a baseline human function.' Katy Bowman, Move Your DNA.
https://www.nutritiousmovement.com/

Fighting Monkey

Dynamic approach to movement, healthy ageing and life-long learning based on research and dialogue between Art, Physical Performance and Effective Communication.
https://fightingmonkey.net/

Rafe Kelley

Rafe's passion is to help people build the physical practice that will help make them the strongest, most adaptable and resilient version of themselves in movement and in life.
https://www.evolvemoveplay.com/rafe-kelley/

Erwan Le Corre

Erwan Le Corre is the founder of MovNat, a synthesis of his long-term passion for real-world physical competency, his love of movement in nature, his extensive knowledge of Physical Education history and his personal philosophy of life. He believes it is everyone's universal and biological birthright to be strong, healthy, happy and free. He calls this state of being our 'True Nature'.
https://www.movnat.com/movnat-team/erwan-le-corre/

Ben Medder

Ben shares his ideas through guided individual movement practice, creative games and tasks to spark the imagination and fuel the muse for reflection, shifting attention between working with your own body, with partners/within a group and interacting and moving through the surrounding environment.
https://www.benmedder.com/

Ido Portal

Most – if not all – 'movement teachers' are really only concerned with a specific discipline, whether that's dance or martial arts or strength training. Ido started to look for someone who was actually interested in the bigger picture of movement, who could look beyond their own disciplines to deal with movement at the highest level. Not being able to find them, Ido decided to become that person.
https://www.idoportal.com

Dr Nicholas Romanov

Developer of the Pose Method® and world-renowned sports scientist. He was born, raised and educated in Russia, but relocated to the United States in the early 1990s. In 2002, alongside Professor Tim Noakes et al., Dr Romanov conducted a groundbreaking scientific study that demonstrated how to reduce, by virtually 50%, the impact on the knees in running.
https://nicholasromanov.com/

Lee Saxby

Over the last 20 years Lee has created educational programs (Wildfitness, Vivobarefoot Training Clinic, Born To Run, MyFoot.com), consulted to shoe companies (TerraPlana/Vivobarefoot, Joe Nimble), participated in university research projects and helped 'unfixable' injured athletes, from recreational runners to Olympians.
https://www.leesaxby.com/

Tom Weksler

Tom believes contemporary dance is the art of reinventing the forms every time he dances, and the practice of synergy between dance and other art forms. He is also very interested in dance outside of the conventions of theatre and in bringing dance to more layers of society, nature and the streets. His embodied philosophy is guided by Zen Buddhism and relates to acting from playfulness and meditation. Martial arts and acrobatics have been his hobbies since childhood and he is constantly inspired by literature, philosophy, animation, architecture, music and cinema.
https://www.movementarchery.com/tom-weksler

Barefoot footwear recommendations

Vivobarefoot
https://www.vivobarefoot.com/uk/

Wild Sole Sandals
https://wildsolesandals.com

Concepts, philosophies and protocols

Scott C. Anderson, PsychoBiotic Revolution

Through various avenues, your microbiota can communicate with your brain. If your microbiota gets out of balance, you can quickly become anxious. If you've ever suffered food poisoning, you know the feeling. This is called dysbiosis, and if you can't shake it, you can end up with chronic inflammation and long-term depression.
http://psychobiotic-revolution.com/

Nadine Artemis

https://int.livinglibations.com/pages/let-the-sun-shine-in

Phillip Beach, Archetypal Postures

To stand up from the floor is a movement sequence we mastered as children. Regrettably, in our busy lives this mastery has lessened over time until the normal act of rising from the floor becomes awkward and uncomfortable. Our musculoskeletal system needs the exercise of erecting to stay in good moving health. I call these the Erectorcises and the ability to relearn and reintroduce these exercises into everyday life provides some protection from degeneration and dis-ease.

https://phillipbeach.com/archetypal-postures/

John Bowlby

British psychiatrist who demonstrated that the nature of our human development and early bonds with our parents plays a crucial role throughout our lives. In *A Secure Base,* Bowlby evidences the ways in which strong emotional ties promote mental health. He illuminates many other aspects of intimate relationships, including fathers' unique roles, the origins of depression in childhood experience and the special communication between psychotherapists and their patients.

Dr Natasha Campbell-McBride, Gut and Psychology Syndrome

When the brain is in trouble it can produce any mixture of symptoms. Gut and Psychology Syndrome (GAPS) addresses the root of all of these symptoms and diseases, including learning disabilities and mental illnesses, such as autism, ADHD/ADD, dyslexia, dyspraxia, addictions, depression, obsessive-compulsive disorder, bipolar disorder, schizophrenia, epilepsy, eating disorders and many other conditions that affect the function of the brain.

https://www.gaps.me/

Robynne Chutkan

Dr Chutkan has helped thousands of patients suffering from a disordered microbiome with her comprehensive Live Dirty, Eat Clean Plan, designed to remove damaging medications and foods, replace important bacteria that have been lost, and restore health. *The Microbiome Solution* offers a microbiome overview, nourishing recipes, questions for your doctor, preventative and recovery health

tips, and the next frontier for a severely troubled microbiome – the stool transplant.
https://www.penguinrandomhouse.com/books/318099/the-microbiome-solution-by-robynne-chutkan/

Nicola Dunn Constellations
An experienced systemic psychotherapist and coach specializing in Constellations Therapy, working with clients on their personal and business relationships, health and creativity.
https://nicoladunnconstellations.com/

Edward Goldsmith
Founder of *The Ecologist* magazine four decades ago, Teddy Goldsmith was instrumental in everything from the setting up of the world's first political green party to being the first to expose many of the problems associated with global development, such as giant dams and nuclear power.
https://theecologist.org/tag/edward-goldsmith

Peter Gray
American psychologist specializing in research work on education and play. Known for *Free to Learn*, his work on how unleashing the instinct to play will make our children happier, more self-reliant and better students for life.

Wim Hof, The Wim Hof Method
Dutch extreme athlete Wim Hof got his nickname 'The Iceman' by breaking a number of records related to cold exposure, including climbing Mount Kilimanjaro in shorts, running a half marathon above the Arctic Circle barefoot, and standing in a container while

covered with ice cubes for more than 112 minutes. Using 'cold, hard nature' as his teacher, his extensive training has enabled him to learn to control his breathing, heart rate and blood circulation and to withstand extreme temperatures.
https://www.wimhofmethod.com/

J. Krishnamurti

This philosopher and religious teacher talked about the problems of living as a human being in society and the need for the individual to free themselves from inner burdens. His book, *As One Is*, published in 1955 and based on several of his lectures, looks at the confusion behind human suffering.
https://jkrishnamurti.org/content/how-one-be-aware-0

Jean Liedloff

According to Jean Liedloff, The Continuum Concept is the idea that, in order to achieve optimal physical, mental and emotional development, human beings – especially babies – require the kind of experience to which our species adapted during the long process of our evolution through countless millennia.
https://continuumconcept.org/summary

Bruce Lipton

Stem cell biologist and bestselling author of *The Biology of Belief*, Dr Lipton made discoveries that ran counter to the established scientific view that life is controlled by genes, giving rise to one of today's most important fields of study: the science of epigenetics. Two major scientific publications derived from these studies defined the molecular pathways connecting the mind and body.
https://www.brucelipton.com/about/

Richard Louv

In his international bestseller *Last Child in the Woods*, Richard Louv spotlights the alienation of children from the natural world, coining the term nature-deficit disorder and outlining the benefits of a strong nature connection – from boosting mental acuity and creativity to reducing obesity and depression, from promoting health and wellness to simply having fun.

http://richardlouv.com/

Gabor Maté

Renowned speaker and bestselling author on trauma, Dr Gabor Maté weaves together scientific research, case histories and his own insights and experience to present a broad perspective that enlightens and empowers people to promote their own healing from addiction, stress and childhood development.

https://drgabormate.com/about/

Robert Moore and Douglas Gillette

In 1992, a Jungian analyst and a mythologist combined to produce a book providing the psychological foundation for a mature, authentic and revitalized masculinity. Based on Carl Jung's four masculine archetypes, *King Warrior Magician Lover* became a bestseller.

https://www.amazon.co.uk/King-Warrior-Magician-Lover-Rediscovering/dp/0062506064

Desmond Morris – *The Human Zoo*

Popular author in zoology and human sociobiology. His books include *The Naked Ape* and *The Human Zoo*.

https://www.amazon.co.uk/Human-Zoo-Desmond-Morris/dp/0099482118

Joseph Chilton Pearce
Grandfather of the Conscious Parenting Movement.
https://josephchiltonpearce.org/

Auguste Rollier
Swiss physician responsible for bringing Heliotherapy to the world in the early 20th century. Published *Heliotherapy* in 1927.
https://www.advancedhealing.com/
auguste-rollier-heliotherapy-then-and-now/

Robert M. Sapolsky
American neuroendocrinology researcher, professor of biology and neurology and author of *Why Zebras Don't Get Ulcers* and *A Primate's Memoir.*

Rudolf Steiner
Austrian scientist and thinker, who used his philosophy around the human as a threefold being of spirit, soul and body to set up Steiner Schools and more. He also founded the biodynamic approach to agriculture, as well as the spiritual-scientific approach to knowledge known as anthroposophy.
https://www.waldorfeducation.org/waldorf-education/
rudolf-steiner-the-history-of-waldorf-education

Isabella Tree
Award-winning author and travel writer, who lives with her husband, the conservationist Charlie Burrell, in the middle of a pioneering rewilding project in West Sussex.
https://www.isabellatree.com/

Daniel Vitalis, WildFed

For 10 years Daniel Vitalis lectured around North America and abroad, offering workshops that helped others lead healthier, more nature-integrated lives. A successful entrepreneur, he founded the nutrition company SurThrival.com in 2008 and headed up a culinary adventure TV series about hunting, fishing, foraging and turning wild ingredients into delicious meals. Most recently, he hosted the popular podcast *ReWild Yourself.*
https://www.danielvitalis.com/

Terry Wahls

The Wahls Protocol® comes out of Dr Wahls' own quest to treat the debilitating symptoms she experiences as a sufferer of progressive MS. Informed by science, she began using paleo principles as guidelines for her unique, nutrient-rich plan. This book shares Dr Wahls' astonishing personal story of recovery and details the programme, with up-to-date research she's now conducting at the University of Iowa.
https://terrywahls.com/

Locations, programmes and campaigns

42 Acres

At its core, 42 Acres continues to invite people to reconnect with nature, self and others but has now grown to offer so much more, including a range of wellbeing and nature-based experiences and events, a biodynamic farm and an abundant nature reserve, to grow and eat in a way that serves the health of people and the planet. We journey well beyond the farm-to-table concept and delve deeper into our soils and our gut. We believe that the soils in which we grow food, and our guts in which the food ends up, are one and the same.

https://www.42acres.com/

Broughton Sanctuary Nature Recovery Programme

A heartfelt commitment to address one of our deepest contemporary crises – our lack of harmonious co-existence with the earth – an issue causing mass extinction of species across the globe as well as a deep lack of belonging for humanity. We feel it is our duty to leave the Broughton Sanctuary in a much healthier condition for generations to come and aim to demonstrate how humans can live in a more fruitful and positive partnership with the land, in a way which helps both nature and humanity to truly flourish.

https://www.broughtonhall.co.uk/nature-recovery

Choose Earth

A campaign driven by Brazilian indigenous leaders fighting for the future of our planet. Facing an extreme human rights, social and climate justice struggle, indigenous communities across Brazil are under a greater threat than ever before. Working alongside indigenous community leaders, activists, journalists, shamans, artists, spiritual leaders, agro-foresters and academics, Choose Earth wants to invest in indigenous strategies, share intelligence and resource the frontline defenders who are protecting life for all.

https://www.chooseearth.co/

Earthrise

Earthrise is a creative studio dedicated to communicating the climate crisis, harnessing the optimism and imagination to build the world we so urgently need.
https://www.earthrise.studio

Knepp Wildland Project

The vision of the Knepp Wildland Project is radically different to conventional nature conservation in that it is not driven by specific goals or target species. Instead, its driving principle is to establish a functioning ecosystem where nature is given as much freedom as possible. The aim is to show how a 'process-led' approach can be a highly effective, low-cost method of ecological restoration – suitable for failing or abandoned farmland – that can work to support established nature reserves and wildlife sites, helping to provide the webbing that will one day connect them together on a landscape scale.
https://knepp.co.uk/home

Survival International

Survival International fights for tribal peoples' survival. They stop loggers, miners and oil companies from destroying tribal lands, lives and livelihoods across the globe. They lobby governments to recognize indigenous land rights. They document and expose the atrocities committed against tribal people and take direct action to stop them. They give tribal peoples a platform to speak to the world. They've had over 200 victories since 1969, but their work is far from over and they need our help.
https://www.survivalinternational.org/

Further reading

Heliotherapy, A. Rollier MD (Oxford Medical Publications, 1923)

The Science of Orgasm, Barry R. Komisaruk et al (John Hopkins University Press, 2006)

The Biology of Belief: Unleashing the Power of Consciousness, Matter and Miracles, Bruce H. Lipton (Hay House, 2005)

The Hunting Apes: Meat Eating and the Origins of Human Behavior, Craig B. Stanford (Princeton University Press, 2001)

Breath: The New Science of a Lost Art, James Nestor (Penguin Life, 2021)

Stealing Fire: How Silicon Valley, the Navy SEALs, and Maverick Scientists are Revolutionizing the Way We Live and Work, Jamie Wheal and Steven Kotler (Dey Street Books, 2017)

Magical Child: Rediscovering Nature's Plan For Our Children, Joseph Chilton Pearce (Penguin, 1992

Why We Sleep: The New Science of Sleep and Dreams, Matthew Walker (Penguin, 2007)

Why Zebras Don't Get Ulcers, Robert M. Sapolsky (St Martin's Press, 2004)

References

Chapter 1

Britt Holewinski, 'Underground Networking: The Amazing Connections Beneath Your Feet', National Forest Foundation. https://www.nationalforests.org/blog/underground-mycorrhizal-network

Richard Grant, 'Do Trees Talk to Each Other?', *Smithsonian Magazine*, March 2018. https://www.smithsonianmag.com/science-nature/the-whispering-trees-180968084/

Claire Marshall, 'Wood wide web: Trees' social networks are mapped', BBC News, 15 May 2019. https://www.bbc.co.uk/news/science-environment-48257315.amp

Q. Li, K. Morimoto, A. Nakadai, H. Inagaki et al, 'Forest bathing enhances human natural killer activity and expression of anti-cancer proteins', *International Journal of Immunopathology and Pharmacology*, April–June 2007, 20(20), 3–8. https://pubmed.ncbi.nlm.nih.gov/17903349/

Chapter 2

Gabor Maté, 'Beyond Drugs: The Universal Experience of Addiction', Dr Gabor Maté. https://drgabormate.com/opioids-universal-experience-addiction/

Rishi Sriram, 'Why Ages 2–7 Matter So Much for Brain Development', *Edutopia*, 24 June 2020. https://www.edutopia.org/article/why-ages-2-7-matter-so-much-brain-development

Craig Gustafson, 'Bruce Lipton, PhD: The Jump From Cell Culture to Consciousness', *Integrative Medicine (Encinitas)*, December 2017, 16(6), 44–50. https://www.ncbi.nlm.nih.gov/pmc/articles/PMC6438088/

Amy Packham, 'Children Around The World Spend Less Time Outdoors Than Prisoners, Global Study Reveals', *Huffington Post*, 22 March 2016. https://www.huffingtonpost.co.uk/amp/entry/children-spend-less-time-outdoors-than-prisoners_uk_56f11f94e4b0fbd4fe087d3a/

Chapter 3

Jonathan Hamill, Jaime Hallak, Serdar M. Dursun, Glen Baker, 'Ayahuasca: Psychological and Physiological Effects, Pharmacology and Potential Uses in Addiction and Mental Illness', *Current Neuropharmacology*, 2019, 17(2), 108–28. https://pubmed.ncbi.nlm.nih.gov/29366418/

Chapter 4

S. T. Telles, R. Nagarathna, H. R. Nagendra, 'Breathing through a particular nostril can alter metabolism and autonomic activities',

Indian Journal of Physiology and Pharmacology, April 1994, 38(2), 133–7. https://pubmed.ncbi.nlm.nih.gov/8063359/

'Effect of western diet on facial and dental development', Lotus Dental, 31 January 2020. https://www.lotusdental.com.au/post/effect-of-western-diet-on-facial-and-dental-development

Baylor College of Medicine, 'Brain circuit connects feeding and mood in response to stress', *Science Daily*, 4 September 2019. https://www.sciencedaily.com/releases/2019/09/190904213722.htm

Manpreet Kaur, Rajinder Kumar Sharma, Shikha Tewar, Satish Chander Narula, 'Influence of mouth breathing on outcome of scaling and root planing in chronic periodontitis', *British Dental Journal Open*, 9 November 2018. https://www.ncbi.nlm.nih.gov/pmc/articles/PMC6226516/

Daniel E. Lieberman, Mickey Mahaffey, Silvino Cubesare Quimare, Nicholas B. Holowka, Ian J. Wallace, Aaron L. Baggish, 'Running in Tarahumara (Rarámuri) Culture', *Current Anthropology*, June 2020, 61(3). https://www.journals.uchicago.edu/doi/pdfplus/10.1086/708810

Megan Teychenne, Lena D. Stephens, Sarah A. Costigan, Dana Lee Olstad, Brendon Stubbs, Anne I. Turner, 'The association between sedentary behaviour and indicators of stress: a systematic review', *BMC Public Health*, 23 October 2019, 19(1), 1357. https://pubmed.ncbi.nlm.nih.gov/31647002/

Chapter 5

Jenneke van Geest, Rosemarie Samaritter, Susan van Hooren, 'Move and Be Moved: The Effect of Moving Specific Movement

Elements on the Experience of Happiness', *Frontiers in Psychology*, 15 January 2021, 11:579518. https://pubmed.ncbi.nlm.nih.gov/33584414/

Hsin-Yu An, Wei Chen, Cheng-Wei Wang et al, 'The Relationships between Physical Activity and Life Satisfaction and Happiness among Young, Middle-Aged, and Older Adults', *International Journal of Environmental Research and Public Health*, July 2020, 17(3), 4817. https://www.ncbi.nlm.nih.gov/pmc/articles/PMC7369812/

Tomasz Cudejko, James Gardiner, Asangaedem Akpan, Kristiaan D'Aout, 'Minimal footwear improves stability and physical function in middle-aged and older people compared to conventional shoes', *Clinical Biomechanics*, January 2020, 71, 139–45. https://www.sciencedirect.com/science/ article/pii/S0268003319304231

Dariush Dfarhud, Maryam Malmir, Mohammad Khanahmadi, 'Happiness & Health: The Biological Factors- Systematic Review Article', *Iranian Journal of Public Health*, November 2014, 43(11), 1468–77. https://www.ncbi.nlm.nih.gov/pmc/articles/PMC4449495/

Chapter 6

Juliana Durack, Susan V. Lynch, 'The gut microbiome: Relationships with disease and opportunities for therapy', *Journal of Experimental Medicine*, 7 January 2019, 216(1), 20–40. https://www.ncbi.nlm.nih.gov/pmc/articles/PMC6314516/

Andrew B. Shreiner, John Y. Kao, Vincent B. Young, 'The gut microbiome in health and in disease', *Current Opinion in Gastroenterology*, January 2015, 31(1), 69–75. https://www.ncbi.nlm.nih.gov/pmc/articles/PMC4290017/

Helen Tremlett, Kylynda C. Bauer, Silke Appel-Cresswell, Brett B. Finlay, Emmanuelle Waubant, 'The gut microbiome in human neurological disease: a review', *Annals of Neurology*, Mar 2017, 81(3), 369–82. https://pubmed.ncbi.nlm.nih.gov/28220542/

Z. X. Tan, R. Lal, K. D. Wiebe, 'Global Soil Nutrient Depletion and Yield Reduction', *Journal of Sustainable Agriculture*, 2006, 26(1), 123–46. https://www.tandfonline.com/doi/abs/10.1300/J064v26n01_1

Samuel A. Smits, Jeff Leach, Erica D. Sonnenburg, Carlos G. Gonzalez et al, 'Seasonal Cycling in the Gut Microbiome of the Hadza Hunter-Gatherers of Tanzania', *Science*, 25 August 2017, 357(6353), 802–806. https://www.ncbi.nlm.nih.gov/pmc/articles/PMC5891123/

Chapter 7

Alina Masters, Seithikurippu R. Pandi-Perumal, Azizi Seixas et al, 'Melatonin, the Hormone of Darkness: From Sleep Promotion to Ebola Treatment', *Brain Disorders & Therapy*, 2014, 4(1), 1000151. https://www.ncbi.nlm.nih.gov/pmc/articles/PMC4334454/

Chapter 8

Paul A. Sandifer, Ariana E. Sutton-Grier, Bethney P. Ward, 'Exploring connections among nature, biodiversity, ecosystem services, and human health and well-being: Opportunities to enhance health and biodiversity conservation', *Ecosystem Services*, April 2015, 12, 1–15. https://www.sciencedirect.com/science/article/pii/S2212041614001648

Faculty of Biological and Environmental Sciences, 'A forest-based yard improved the immune system of daycare children in only a month', University of Helsinki, 14 October 2020. https://www.helsinki.fi/en/faculty-biological-and-environmental-sciences/news/forest-based-yard-improved-immune-system-daycare-children-only-month

Marja I. Roslund, Riikka Puhakka, Mira Grönroos, Noora Nurminen et al, 'Biodiversity intervention enhances immune regulation and health-associated commensal microbiota among daycare children', *Science Advances*, 14 October 2020, 6(42). https://www.science.org/doi/10.1126/sciadv.aba2578

Melanie Rüger, Marijke C. M. Gordijn, Domien G. M. Beersma, Bonnie de Vries, Serge Daan, 'Time-of-day-dependent effects of bright light exposure on human psychophysiology: comparison of daytime and nighttime exposure', *American Journal of Physiology – Regulatory, Integrative and Comparative Physiology*, May 2006, 290(5), R1413–20. https://pubmed.ncbi.nlm.nih.gov/16373441/

Index

Acknowledgements

I dedicate this book to you, Katarina: my rock, my lover, my best friend, the wisest adviser and the phenomenal mother to our four wildlings that you are. Katarina, thank you for seeing in me the being I needed to become and holding the space for my 'Be More Human' experience to unravel. You are loved.

I dedicate this book to my four wildlings: Lola, Millie, Tallulah and Bow – thank you for choosing me to be your papa; for being my wisest teachers; for unveiling my papa powers; for inspiring me to dismantle and deconstruct the templates of the old Tony 1.0 and ultimately shining your bright lights on the path to discovering the wild, connected empowered version of me.

Without my tribe of influence this book certainly would not be where it is today. It may have my name on the front cover, but the writing process has been so much more than an independent effort. I am truly grateful to all of you for your experiences, wisdom, love and support in shaping this – from those that that have coached me, held space for me and with me, heard me and held me, held up a mirror and flagged up my BS and to those of you that first planted the 'you should write a book' seeds.

Thank you to my agent Valeria Huerta for believing those 'you should write a book' seeds would grow, and for watering them behind the scenes. Thank you to Minty Mint, Rachel Bednarski and Mark Griffiths for all your magical help shaping words and helping me discover the writer within.

Thank you to Emily Robertson for embracing my 'Be More Human' vision, Anya Hayes for picking up the baton, and the Penguin Life team of incredible editors for helping me find the confidence to tap away at my laptop for what felt like an eternity.

And finally . . . I dedicate this book to you and hope it speaks to the wild, connected and empowered version of you and inspires you to take on the all-important personal and planetary change for all of our children's children.